MORE THAN
MEETS *the* EYE

MORE THAN MEETS *the* EYE

FASCINATING GLIMPSES *of* GOD'S POWER AND DESIGN

RICHARD A. SWENSON, M.D.

NAVPRESS®

Bringing Truth to Life

OUR GUARANTEE TO YOU

We believe so strongly in the message of our books that
we are making this quality guarantee to you. If for any
reason you are disappointed with the content of this book,
return the title page to us with your name and address and
we will refund to you the list price of the book. To help us
serve you better, please briefly describe why you were
disappointed. Mail your refund request to: NavPress, P.O.
Box 35002, Colorado Springs, CO 80935.

NAVPRESS
P.O. Box 35001
Colorado Springs, CO 80935

The Navigators is an international Christian organization. Our mission is to reach, disciple, and equip people
to know Christ and to make Him known through successive generations. We envision multitudes of diverse
people in the United States and every other nation who have a passionate love for Christ, live a lifestyle of
sharing Christ's love, and multiply spiritual laborers among those without Christ.

NavPress is the publishing ministry of The Navigators. NavPress publications help believers learn
biblical truth and apply what they learn to their lives and ministries. Our mission is to stimulate
spiritual formation among our readers.

Cover design by David Carlson Design
Cover photos by Digital Stock
Creative Team: Jacqueline Eaton Blakley, Lisa Sheltra, Lori Mitchell, and Tim Howard

Some of the anecdotal illustrations in this book are true to life and are included with the permission of the
persons involved. All other illustrations are composites of real situations, and any resemblance to people
living or dead is coincidental.

Unless otherwise identified, all Scripture quotations in this publication are taken from the HOLY BIBLE:
NEW INTERNATIONAL VERSION® (NIV®). Copyright © 1973, 1978, 1984 by International Bible Society.
Used by permission of Zondervan Publishing House. All rights reserved. Other versions used include: the
Revised Standard Version Bible (RSV), copyright 1946, 1952, 1971, by the Division of Christian Education of
the National Council of the Churches of Christ in the USA, used by permission, all rights reserved; *The New
English Bible* (NEB), © 1961, 1970, The Delegates of the Oxford University Press and The Syndics of the
Cambridge University Press; and the *King James Version* (KJV).

Library of Congress Cataloging-in-Publication Data

Swenson, Richard A.
        More than meets the eye : fascinating glimpses of God's power and design / Richard A. Swenson.
            p. cm.
        Includes bibliographical references and index.
        ISBN 1-57683-069-1
            1. God--Omnipotence. I. Title.
BT133 .S94 2000
231'.4--dc21   00-056255

Printed in the United States of America
5 6 7 8 9 10 11 12 13 / 10 09 08 07 06

FOR A FREE CATALOG OF
NAVPRESS BOOKS & BIBLE STUDIES,
CALL 1-800-366-7788 (USA)
OR 1-800-839-4769 (CANADA)

Dedicated to
all those who find themselves drawn into
the mysterious depths of God

Let's go there together

CONTENTS

ACKNOWLEDGMENTS

Any such book effort represents the convergence of many influences that ought to be appropriately acknowledged. Carter and Curtis Folkestad permitted the extended use of important resource materials. Bill and Gail Thedinga, Dr. Roger and Joanne Natwick, Sue Harrison, and Helen Olechno contributed books and articles. Over years of presenting this content to varied audiences, many people have offered resources and ideas that further stimulated my thinking.

Don Steffen, David and Debbie Bochman, Jack and Diana Stimmel reviewed portions of the text at my request and offered helpful advice. Diana Stimmel, in particular, gave a thoughtful reading of the first seven chapters and offered important scriptural insights.

The physics faculty at Denison University stimulated me in this direction years ago, and Dr. Rod Grant has continued to do so with his important book on medical physics. In addition, Dr. Fuz Rana kindly gave assistance on an uncertain physics question.

Dr. Charles and Becky Folkestad provided medical resources, as did Dr. Scott Wright of the Mayo Clinic. Both my head and my heart thank you.

Darlene Bochman provided her exceptional secretarial skills. Many others contributed practical encouragement: among them Opal Harstad, Paul and Comfort Attah, and Hazel Bent. Our extended families, as always, have given continuous support.

I wish to thank NavPress for their dedicated attention to this text. Once again, heartfelt gratitude to editor Don Simpson for his wise expertise and gentle guidance.

My wife Linda—who has both English and R.N. degrees—continues to function as an invaluable researcher, scholarly advisor, and copy editor. I can't even begin to imagine doing this kind of research and writing without her assistance, which extends into many thousands of hours of work. In writing as in life, it is an honor to work side-by-side with such a gifted person. To our sons Matt and Adam (and now Maureen!)—thanks for listening to the ideas, enhancing the discussions, understanding the deadlines . . . and thanks simply for patiently being our beloved children.

A NEW VISION *of* POWER

Week after week we witness the same miracle: that God is so mighty he can stifle his own laughter. . . . Does anyone have the foggiest idea what sort of power we so blithely invoke?[1]

ANNIE DILLARD is right. And she is right in a way that should stop us all in our tracks. In every square millimeter of her thought there is a ton of implication.

God's power is undeniable; His precision is impressive; His sovereignty is on display. Why then do we live in such a metaphysical stupor? How can such power fail to dominate our every thought and action?

It is not that God has failed to clearly demonstrate His nature, or that He has been lax in instructing us. It is just that we are slow to understand. Our eyesight is dim. This world is too much with us.

What we need is a new vision of God. The real God. Not some vague image we fold up and stuff in the back drawer of life, but the kind of God who parts the Red Sea and shakes Mount Sinai. The kind of God who stuns the physicists with symmetry, the mathematicians with precision, the engineers with design, the politicians with power, and the poets with beauty.

I often try to imagine what it would be like to cross into eternity for just ten minutes and sit in the presence of God. If we could do that and then return to live out our lives, what would change? Everything. And the change would be complete.

What might such a visit be like?

TEN MINUTES IN HEAVEN

Dick: Do you really know everything, God?

God: Do you doubt it?

Dick: Well, no. But how do you do it? Doesn't it get kind of mixed up in your head?

God: I think you are getting the two of us confused. Let me put it this way. Things often get mixed up and chaotic in *your* head, but not in mine. Dick, my car never runs out of gas. I've never been late for a plane. And when you try to balance your checkbook . . . I can't even bear to watch. So I distract myself by counting backwards to infinity.

Dick: Well, tell me something you know about me that I don't know about myself.

God: You have forty-two thousand fewer neurons in the right side of your brain than the left. You have 18.755 billion trillion air molecules in your lungs right now. You have a sixth cousin who is a plumber in Sundsvall, Sweden. And the rear passenger-side tire of your Chevy is a little low. Want me to keep going?

Dick: You've got to be kidding! You keep track of things like that?

God: Of course. I don't even try. It is all a part of omniscience. I know absolutely everything about you.

Dick: Could I see you answer some prayers?

God: Of course.

Dick: When?

God: I just did.

Dick: What?

God: I just answered prayers.

Dick: Whose prayer did you answer?

God: Actually, I answered 924,338 prayers just then. Half of the people didn't even realize it. That happens often.

   A high percentage of the prayers I answer are not even from adults. It's the kids, you know. They are the ones with the faith. When I answer their prayers, they usually see it right away.

Dick: What percentage of the prayers you just answered were from kids?

God: 42.57688493005998 . . . how many decimals do you want?

Dick: OK. I get the point.

God: That was the best thing I ever did.

Dick: What? Answer those prayers?

God: No. Make kids. Kids are the greatest. They "perfect praise." Do you know that verse? Never mind.

Back at creation one of the angels suggested I just make everybody adults straightaway. You know—skip the teenage thing. But the angel was wrong. Kids are great.

Dick: Could you tell me the names of all the stars?

God: Yes I could. But you only have ten minutes.

Dick: What about the galaxies, then?

God: As I said, you only have ten minutes.

Do you want to see me annihilate a galaxy? We have time for that.

Dick: Sure!

God: See that galaxy way out there, toward the edge of space? It hasn't even been discovered yet. No one will miss it. I just made it because I liked the way it sparkles. . . .

There. Can't see the galaxy now, can you?

Dick: That was some explosion! How did you do that?

God: Have you ever heard of antimatter? Maybe you don't want to know—it would probably give you mightmares.

Dick: Do you mean nightmares?

God: I *know* what I mean. I mean mightmares. I just invented the word.

Dick: I'm a physician, you know.

God: Is that supposed to impress me? I'm a Physician too. Want to compare credentials? Success rates?

Dick: One of my patients died last week. She was an older woman from the nursing home; her name was Katherine. She was ready to go. Can you tell me if she is OK?

God: I know Katherine well. She's fine—never felt better. I don't know why people are so hesitant to leave Earth. Once they cross the line, I heal them instantly. I love doing it. They love it too.

Dick: How much of my ten minutes do I have left?

God: Just a few seconds. Of course, around here that might also mean fifty thousand years. You never know. But in your case, it means just a few seconds.

Dick: Do you watch me when I'm down there?

God: All the time.

Dick: I don't know if that's frightening or comforting.

God: It's both.

Dick: Medicine is getting rather stressful these days.

God: I noticed.

Dick: What should I do about it?

God: I'm glad you asked. One thing that would help a lot is if you were to stop using me as a last resort. Everything you need, I've already provided. Trust me. Use my wisdom and power. Pray. Dick, you really ought to pray more. And love your patients. On your best days, I'll give you great joy. And on your worst days, I'll get you through it. I will *always* get you through it.

Dick: Thanks. I guess there's no pretending to you that I need a lot of help.

God: Yes, it's no use pretending. A great many people try to pretend with me, but it hasn't worked yet and I see no reason to suspect you will have any better success.

Dick: One last question: I am fifty-two years old. How much longer am I going to live?

God: Do you mean in earth time or heaven time?

Dick: Either. Both.

God: I won't tell you in earth time. You will just have to leave that to me. In heaven time, you have a vapor's length of time left.

Dick: That sounds kind of scary.

God: No, it sounds biblical. See you in a vapor. And remember, everything you need I've already provided. Trust me.

LIVING AWARE

We can't exactly go to the other side and sit with God for ten minutes. But we can know a lot more about Him than we have previously settled for. The Scriptures help build our understanding of God's sovereignty on a practical level—by that, I mean the kind of knowledge that affects our everyday behavior. But science is also a fascinating source of revelation, and increasingly so.

The scientific facts presented in this book are impossible to dismiss. They are a stick of dynamite under the front porch of our spiritual complacency. When we lift up any stone of the universe, God's fingerprints stare back at us. Everything is there, waiting to be discovered. All the evidence we need, and more. "I love to think of nature as an unlimited broadcasting station, through which God speaks to us every hour, if we will only tune in," said George Washington Carver.[2]

"We are living in a world that is absolutely transparent, and God is shining through it all the time," said Thomas Merton. "That is not just a fable or a nice story. It is true. If we abandon ourselves to God and forget ourselves, we see it sometimes, and we see it maybe frequently. God shows Himself everywhere, in everything—in people, and in things and in nature and in events. It becomes very obvious that God is everywhere and in everything and we cannot be without Him. It's impossible. The only thing is that we don't see it."[3]

When we understand the sovereignty, power, design, majesty, precision, genius, intimacy, and caring of an Almighty God, it takes away our fear. It removes our frustration. It allows us to sleep at night and trust Him with the running of His own universe. It allows us to have margin. It allows us to resume our proper role in the order of things rather than taking over His role. It allows us to seek His will rather than follow our own mind.

The more we understand about God's power, the less we worry about our weakness. The more we trust in God's sovereignty, the less we fret about our future. "There is no attribute more comforting to His children," said Charles Spurgeon, "than God's sovereignty."[4]

WHAT KIND OF POWER?

This is a book about science. On a deeper level, this is a book about the design of science. As you read, it is my hope that you will be fascinated by the science, and captivated by the Designer who stands behind it all.

But know this: the God described in this book is uncontrollable. You will come to see Him, but only on His terms. He will give you rest, but only after He has shaken the foundations of your life.

What kind of Power do we so blithely invoke? He spoke the universe into existence. Nothingness obeys His voice. He controls time, space, matter, and light. He monitors the position of every elementary particle. He is sufficient unto Himself. He does not need anybody or anything to accomplish His purposes. He answers to no one. He obeys only His own counsel. He works on thousands of levels all at the same time. His scientific sophistication is unfathomable. He created the laws of physics, and appears to be a "pure mathematician."[5] His intelligence is so superior, according to Einstein, that in comparison "all the systematic thinking and acting of human beings is an utterly insignificant reflection."[6]

Look up the word *omnipotent.* Either He is or He isn't. And if He is, we had better prepare ourselves to accept the consequences. "It is madness to wear ladies' straw hats and velvet hats to church," concludes Dillard. "We should all be wearing crash helmets. Ushers should issue life preservers and signal flares; they should lash us to our pews."[7]

You have been warned. So open your mind, open your heart, and may you never recover.

CHAPTER ONE

OUR BODY *in* PARTICLES

W HEN God set out to create humanity He put His genius on display. If we wish to learn more about His ingenuity, precision, and yes, perhaps even His sense of humor, we don't have to go any further than the mirror. The pinnacle of creation, He made us "a little lower than the angels" and crowned us "with glory and honor."[1] As a scientist with training in both medicine and physics, it is easily apparent to me that the majesty of God is revealed in the human body. His fingerprints are, in fact, all over us.

Atoms, Etc.
The human body contains 10^{28} atoms (1 followed by 28 zeros).[2] The universe itself contains perhaps only 10^{20} stars (estimates range as high as 10^{24}). In light of such comparisons, I teach young doctors that the human body is a million times more complex than the universe. Before you get too puffed by it all, understand that a cat has 10^{26} atoms and thus is also more complex than the universe—and don't they know it.[3]

According to isotope studies, 90 percent of our atoms are replaced annually. Every five years, 100 percent of our atoms turn over and become new atoms. Aren't you glad that doesn't hurt?

Aren't you glad your doctor can't charge for it? (Perhaps those are redundant questions.)

In the last hour, one *trillion trillion* of your atoms have been replaced. If all the people on the earth were to set about counting this rate of atomic turnover in your body, each person would have to count ten billion atoms per second to keep up. (By the way, even though we can measure atoms, no one has actually "seen" an atom—perhaps making them even harder to count.)

Who is watching over this atomic exchange? You? Your physician? Only God can monitor something of this magnitude—a process that causes such dramatic exchange and disruption, yet holds all things together.[4] "We speak of the body as a machine, but it is hardly necessary to say that none of the most ingenious machines set up by modern science can for a moment compare with it," observes Scottish biologist Sir J. Arthur Thomson. "The body is a self-building machine; a self-stoking, self-regulating, self-repairing machine—the most marvelous and unique automatic mechanism in the universe."[5]

Genesis explains how we will one day return to the ground, "since from it you were taken; for dust you are and to dust you will return."[6] Naturally, we thought this verse referred to the end of life. In reality the verse is true every moment of every day, even in our healthiest moments. "We are continually being recreated from dust and returning to dust," explains David M. Baughan, M.D. "We are not objects or machines that endure, we are patterns that have the capacity to perpetuate ourselves. We are not things; instead we are processes."[7] Said Buckminster Fuller: "I seem to be a verb."

"Life is a wave, which in no two consecutive moments of its existence is composed of the same particles," explains another physicist, John Tyndall.[8] The fundamental particles that comprise us have been floating around since the beginning. They roost within us for a while, and then move on down the road to inhabit our neighbor. Some of the atoms that resided within our childhood frames are now probably doing their similar work within a body in Mongolia.

"The body is more like a flame than a lump of clay, burning

yet not consumed," says author George Leonard. "The substance of which it is made changes. The essential form persists."[9] This might sound suspiciously New Age, but it is actually pretty good physics. Yes, our bodies are indeed discrete units. But we also leak, both physically and metaphysically. In consequence, we share our physical existence with our neighbors, however remote. Red and yellow, black and white—they are me and I am them. Through shared sneezes, sloughed skin, the jet stream, flowing rivers, and a myriad of other mixing devices, God brings us together constantly.

The Subatomic Level
Of course there are additional organizational units other than atoms. Each level is miraculous in its own right. From the smallest to the largest, we are constructed of:

subatomic particles ➡ atoms ➡ molecules ➡ cells ➡ tissues ➡ organs ➡ systems

When we first discovered the subatomic particles of the proton, neutron, and electron, we thought we had identified the fundamental building blocks of all of nature—surely nothing could be smaller. But scientists sometimes have a way of being premature with their pronouncements, and since then we have identified over 200 subatomic particles smaller than the initial proton, neutron, and electron.

One such subatomic particle is called the *Xi*. It has a life span of one ten-billionth of a second. In the amount of time it takes my heart to beat, this one subatomic particle has gone through billions of lifetimes. Why did God make a Xi? Perhaps He was just having fun, and thought "This will keep a few thousand scientists busy for a decade just trying to track this ghost."

After digging even deeper and uncovering still more particles, some physicists began to speculate that we are infinite—not only in the eternal direction—but also in the subatomic direction. Science devises new and sophisticated technology to penetrate ever smaller levels, only to find yet another little critter winking mischievously at our machines. Other scientists believe that beneath the tiny subatomic "quarks," perhaps the newly postulated superstrings might represent the final bottom of the well. Personally, I believe we are indeed "infinite in all directions."

The Cellular Level

Mix together these subatomic particles, add a bit of mysticism, and out pop some *atoms*. Take about twenty of the most common elemental atoms—especially carbon, oxygen, hydrogen, nitrogen, phosphorus, and sulfur, which account for 99 percent of the dry weight of every living thing—add a bit of mysticism, and out pop some pretty sophisticated *molecules*.[10] Organize molecules in just the right way, add a bit of mysticism, and—this is the really tricky part—out pop some living *cells*.

Not only are the *subatomic particles* flashing in and out of existence faster than a New York cabby changes lanes; not only are the *atoms* turning over at a rate exceeding a billion trillion per second; and not only are the *molecules* continuously rearranging themselves in a dance we might call the nanosecond shuffle . . . but, you guessed it, the *cells* are doing the same thing. It is almost as if God, working at the speed of light, is continuously tinkering with His invention. When Paul wrote: "Though outwardly we are wasting away, yet inwardly we are being renewed day by day,"[11] apparently he was correct on both the spiritual and the physical levels.

The body contains between 10 and 100 trillion cells (and each cell contains approximately a trillion atoms). These cells, like just about everything else in the body, are continually being torn down, remodeled, and replaced. Think of it like this: If your body were a house, and the house were the size of Texas, imagine knocking down the walls in a million rooms every second and hastily rebuilding them again with new materials.

Every couple of days we replace all the cells that line the intestine—faster if we eat Mexican food. Every couple of weeks we replace all the cells of the skin—where did you think all that house dust comes from? Every seven years we replace the entire skeleton.

Different cell types have differing life spans. Many cells last less than a day. Platelets live only a couple of days. Red blood cells live four months. Certain muscle cells can live for years. And nerve cells can live a hundred years. But all cells eventually die. Some die from injury, some from disease, but most die from a form of suicide called *programmed cell death*.

The mystery of cell function is both stunning and inspiring:

- Each cell is unimaginably complex. Each must live in community with its surrounding neighbors, doing its own specialized part in the whole.
- Each cell is surrounded by a membrane thinner than a spider's web that must function precisely or the cell will die.
- Each cell generates its own electric field, which at times is larger than the electric field near a high-voltage power line.[12]
- Each cell contains specialized energy factories called *biofires* that use adenosine triphosphate (ATP). Every cell contains hundreds of these miniature ATP motors embedded in the surfaces of the mitochondria. Each motor is 200 thousand times smaller than a pinhead. At the center of ATP synthase is a tiny wheel that turns at about a hundred revolutions per second and produces three ATP molecules per rotation.[13]
- Cells don't stockpile ATP but instead make it as needed from food consumed. Active people can produce their body weight in ATP every day.[14]
- Each cell has its own internal clock, switching on and off in cycles from two to twenty-six hours, never varying.[15]

If after glimpsing the activity, intricacy, balance, and precision of life at this level you do not suspect a God standing behind it all, then my best diagnostic guess is that you are in a metaphysical coma.

If God put this all together, He must be very clever. And powerful. And precise. Does He know the position of all of these subatomic particles, all the time—even when they come in and out of existence in less than a trillionth of a second? Yes, He does. Not only does He know where they are at all times, but He nicknames them in His spare time.

The point is: such a God can be trusted with the details of my life. After rearranging subatomic particles all morning, the specifics of my life probably seem a bit unchallenging to Him.

CHAPTER TWO

The HEART, BLOOD, *and* LUNGS

POWERING the circulatory system is a formidable task, unforgiving of errors. But the heart is remarkably effective. Every day, uncomplaining, this ten-ounce muscle contracts 100 thousand times nary "missing a beat." Over a lifetime of faithful service, these two self-lubricating, self-regulating, high-capacity pumps beat two and one-half billion times and pump sixty million gallons of blood without pausing to rest. (Technically this is not correct, for the pumping action actually takes place in less than one-third of the cardiac cycle.[1] Even though the heart spends two-thirds of its life resting, the word "lazy" doesn't apply. It takes a rest, but it never takes a vacation.)

A mere three weeks after conception, a sheet of electrically excitable cells organize themselves into an immature heart and begin beating (the first rock band?). At fourteen weeks this heart is already pumping seven gallons per day — compared to two thousand gallons a day for the adult. Solomon wrote that God has "set eternity in the hearts of men; yet they cannot fathom what God has done from beginning to end."[2] I suspect God set that eternity in the heart while still in the womb, but as predicted we did not "fathom what God has done."

This circulatory effort is so dynamic that each blood cell returns back to its cardiac starting place every minute. The 120-day life span of a red blood cell isn't all that glamorous—it runs around in a circle 200,000 times only to be squished by the spleen on its 200,001st trip. Bummer. Not that the little critter should "worry" about it all, for researchers have discovered that worry is bad for the heart.[3] It turns out that when God said, "do not fret,"[4] "do not worry about tomorrow,"[5] and "do not be anxious,"[6] He was acting in His capacity as the world's premier cardio-psychiatrist.

Even though the four-chambered heart is remarkably *effective*, as with all engines it is not mechanically very *efficient* (typically less than 10 percent efficiency rating).[7] Personally, I have no complaints. Any lack of efficiency is more than made up for by a commensurate faithfulness. I stand in awe.

Blood Vessels

The body has sixty thousand miles of blood vessels, a distance nearly two and one-half times around the earth at the equator. This extensive system of branching vessels begins with the large aorta. Blood surges through the aortic valve and out of the left ventricle at high speed and under significant pressure. The high pressures in the arteries then appropriately decrease over the course of flow so important exchanges of oxygen, nutrition, and waste can take place. Once the blood reaches its capillary destination, the express train must slow to a local commuter pace, allowing these passengers to get off and on.

Figure 1—Mean pressures in mm Hg for blood vessels			
Arterial	Capillary, arterial end	Capillary, venous end	Venous
120	30	10	5

The capillaries are so small their average diameter is the same size as a red blood cell (RBC). This means that RBCs often must flow through in single file and sometimes even distort themselves to fit. The capillary wall contains pores that permit the exchange of various molecules, such as water, glucose, electrolytes, oxygen, carbon dioxide, and small proteins. The RBCs themselves can't escape through the capillary wall unless the wall membrane is injured. In that case, however, RBCs spill into the tissues "bruising" them. The wall of the capillary is so delicate it would rupture under a tension one three-thousandth of that required to tear toilet tissue.[8]

If we cut through a cross section of active muscle and put it under a microscope, we would find 190 capillaries in every square millimeter. (A square millimeter is slightly more than one-thousandth of a square inch.) The entire body has about seventy thousand square feet of capillary wall, a figure so large it even dwarfs Bill Gates's fifty thousand square foot house. This large surface area grants the body the abundant room necessary for the exchange of nutrition, oxygen, and waste.

Red Blood Cells

Red blood cells, also known as erythrocytes, are of critical importance to life. "The life is in the blood" is not only good theology but also good biology.[9] The story begins with the critical nature of oxygen. All fires require oxygen, including the energy-releasing fire within our cells. Our problem is that the oxygen is "out there" and not "in here."

In response, God devised a series of ingenious mechanisms to transport oxygen into the tissues. When oxygen is inhaled into the respiratory tract, it snuggles up against the thinner-than-paper lining of the lung wall. Immediately on the other side of this wall are capillaries. The favorable diffusion coefficient attracts the oxygen molecule across the lining and into the capillary blood stream. This diffusion is so successful, however, that the blood stream now has a new problem—a numbers problem. The oxygen molecules, like teenagers offered free pizza, are showing up in the trillions. Since oxygen is not very soluble in blood, they can't all fit into the blood stream and transfer down to the peripheral tissues by simply swimming on their own. An efficient transport system is obviously necessary. God, thinking ahead, ordered up a limo. Actually, an entire fleet. Enter the RBC.

If the body had to depend on the oxygen that was dissolved

in the blood stream, the heart would have to pump twenty-five times as much to accomplish oxygenation of the tissues. God must have thought that represented a lot of unnecessary work, so He invented the RBC. And within each RBC He placed hemoglobin. Hemoglobin is an interesting and complex iron-rich molecule. It has been calculated that the chance that amino acids would line up randomly to create the first hemoglobin protein is 1 in 10^{850}.[10] Not good odds if you were to stake your bet on randomness over design.

The oxygen molecules pile into the RBC limousine by combining with the hemoglobin. Because of the hemoglobin molecule's tremendous affinity for oxygen, each RBC can carry a million molecules of oxygen. Once full, the limo heads down the road in search of hypoxic oxygen-starved cells. Arriving in the capillaries, the RBCs slow to single file. The generous hemoglobin molecules, seeing poor gasping cells on the other side of the capillary wall, release their oxygen. Then, lonely and depressed, the RBC and its desaturated hemoglobin head back to the lungs in search of an oxygen refill.

It is interesting to note that the body believes in leaving a margin. Under normal resting conditions, the RBC releases only about 25 percent of its oxygen to the tissues. This leaves abundant margin for surging to 100 percent—and even beyond—should the need arise during strenuous work and exercise.[11]

Red blood cells are tiny but plentiful. We each make over two million RBCs every second. If we looked at them under a microscope they would look like tiny red donuts. If we took them all out of our body and laid them side by side they would go around the earth at the equator four times.

I wonder if God paused when deciding to create red blood cells . . . realizing that His Son would die by shedding them. How much blood did Christ actually shed? We have no way of knowing for sure. But without a doubt, He shed at least one red blood cell for every human who ever lived.[12] Mathematically He would have accomplished that in His first few drops. And a drop—even a single cell—of such divine blood is sufficient to pay the price of our ransom.

The heart and the blood. There is something deep for us here. It is not a matter of biology but rather of eternity. "Oh, that their hearts would be inclined to fear me and keep all my commands always," God told Moses, "so that it might go well with them and their children forever!"[13]

White Blood Cells, Platelets, and the Immune System

The red blood cells are superstars—but they aren't the real heroes. That award appropriately goes to the white blood cells and platelets. They die for us. They were born ready to die.

Platelets are half the size of erythrocytes and survive only a matter of days. This is why we must continually produce five million new platelets every second. They are critical for the clotting of the blood, rushing to the site of injury and heroically throwing their tiny bodies into the hole.

The white blood cells are no less self-sacrificing. They are a vital link in our quest for daily survival. Not to be paranoid about it but there are billions of microbes continuously seeking to do us harm. This is why the body must have ready fifty billion white blood cells standing guard. These are the active duty forces. But in the reserves, hiding in the bone marrow, we have a backup force one hundred times as large should the need arise.[14]

These microbes are most often either bacteria or viruses. Bacteria—such as strep or staph—live only a matter of minutes but reproduce rapidly by the millions. They are the most prolific form of life on the planet "and if allowed to go unchecked for only thirty-six hours they would reproduce in numbers that could cover the entire planet 'to the thickness of over a foot.'"[15] They are all over us—on the skin, in the gastrointestinal tract, and in the respiratory tract. Many of them are beneficial, and, as a matter of fact, we would not be able to live without them. Others are noxious, while still others can be fatal.

Viruses—such as the cold and flu viruses, measles, and HIV—are different. They are a hundred times smaller than bacteria, averaging one ten-millionth of an inch in diameter. Viruses show no lifelike activity until they occupy a living host cell. They cannot be treated with antibiotics.

The skin and mucosa of the respiratory tract are the first line of defense against microbial attack. Yet should any infectious agents breach this outer defense, the immune system takes over. Here the white blood cell is an important player.

The immune system is extremely complex. Its first responsibility is to identify whether the suspicious invader is friend or foe—that is, is it our own tissue or is it foreign material? Sometimes the immune system makes a tragic, and occasionally fatal, mistake in identification and launches an all-out offensive against the host tissue itself (called an *autoimmune disease,* such as rheumatoid arthritis).

In most cases, however, the immune system plays its role properly. When a foreign agent is identified, a fleet of white blood cells, possessing as many as 100 billion molecular receptors, must perform a vast program of pattern recognition.[16] Antibodies are formed, which then attach themselves to the enemy agents, marking them for destruction.

Next time you get a sore throat, swollen lymph nodes, or inflammation, remember that your body is doing battle on your behalf. Don't be irritated by the fever or discomfort. Instead, just think about the billions of white blood cells that are dying so that you may live.

In some ways, our white blood cells are better Christians than we are. These cells have one mission, one purpose—to give their lives in defense of ours. "Greater love has no one than this," Jesus explained, "that he lay down his life for his friends."[17] Jesus did it for us; our white blood cells and platelets do it for us. Why do we doubt His vigilance when He so faithfully performs it on the microscopic level every day of our lives? The evidence is overwhelming—He sees, He cares, and He defends.

Lungs and Oxygen

Every breath we take contains 150 million molecules that were breathed by Jesus Christ. Yes, that is *every* breath, and 150 *million* molecules.[18] It is one of the many ways He intimately shares life with us. If ever we think we are doing something in secret away from the presence of God, it would probably be fitting to hold our breath while doing so. For whenever we inhale, Jesus is there with us sharing Himself minute by minute and molecule by molecule.

I like to think of it as Jesus performing a kind of mouth-to-mouth resuscitation on us. Daniel spoke of the God who holds your breath in His hand.[19] It perhaps harkens all the way back to the beginning, when God formed the man and "breathed into his nostrils the breath of life."[20]

We breathe about twenty-three thousand times per day and 630 million times over an average life span. With each inhalation we breathe in 10^{22} molecules, more than a billion trillion with each lungful. This amounts to twenty-two pounds of air per day (and no, that is not why your bathroom scale reads heavier).

With the air now in the lungs, the next step is to get it into the bloodstream. To accomplish this, the lungs first divide the breath into smaller portions and send each down a series of dividing wind tunnels. Finally the air arrives into different peripheral rooms where each molecule of oxygen can receive individual attention.

These "rooms," called *alveoli*, are actually tiny air sacs. Perhaps you can picture them like bubbles, miniature balloons, or clusters of hollow grapes. The average diameter of these alveoli is only twice the thickness of paper.[21] Overall, we have about 300 million alveoli, greatly increasing the surface area available for the oxygen to come into contact with. In fact, if you were to spread out the entire alveolar surface and lay it down on the floor, it would equal half the size of a tennis court.

With the inhaled oxygen now closely approximated to the lining of the alveoli, the red blood cells and hemoglobin within the capillaries can attract the oxygen across the thin membrane and begin transporting it to the various cells. The efficiency with which this happens is a measure of our physical fitness. With increased exercise the muscles need more oxygen, and they need it quickly. Under strenuous conditions, the muscle demand for oxygen may increase as much as tenfold. Well-conditioned athletes have an oxygen delivery and utilization mechanism that is more highly efficient than the rest of ours. Yet the capacity to improve our oxygen factory output through exercise is something within the reach of us all regardless of age.

Lack of oxygen leads to death, whether for individual cells, organs, or the entire body. The brain is heavily dependent on oxygen, and catastrophic consequences can happen after even a few minutes of oxygen deprivation.

One interesting medical technique sometimes used in neurosurgery is to cool the brain, thus slowing its oxygen metabolism. Another illustration of that same principle occurs in cold water drowning. In Wisconsin winters, if someone drowns by falling through the ice, we don't consider the person dead until he or she is "warm and dead." Remarkable recoveries have occurred even after thirty minutes of immersion in icy water.

Oxygen is the major player in the respiration scenario—but not the only one. Carbon dioxide (CO_2) must also be removed from the cells, transported to the lungs, and exhaled. Ironically, when people hyperventilate they can remove too much CO_2. That is why the treatment for hyperventilation is breathing into a paper bag, thus rebreathing our own carbon dioxide.

As marvelous as the lungs are, God has mixed in a few other tricks, almost as a sideshow for our entertainment.

- The average speed of a sneeze is sixty-eight miles per hour (mph).
- Each sneeze can contain as many as five thousand droplets that can travel as far as twelve feet.
- The highest speed of sneeze-expelled droplets is 104 mph.
- The longest sneezing fit ever recorded in the *Guinness Book of World Records* is 977 days.
- The longest recorded bout of hiccups is sixty-eight years.
- Adults can produce one quart of respiratory mucus per day.
- The lung cilia that sweep the mucus up the trachea (the lungs' "escalator") vibrate one thousand times per minute.

Once again, God has pulled off another display of His creative genius. All He asks in return is, "everything that has breath praise the LORD."[22]

CHAPTER THREE

The SENSES

"COME to your senses and stop sinning," Paul told the Corinthian church.[1] I don't want to take inappropriate liberties with the text and language, but where does this commonly used phrase "come to your senses" come from? What do people mean by it? Apparently it means *Wake up! Quit kidding yourselves. See with eyes that see, hear with ears that hear.*

The five senses do this for us. Without vision we would not be able to see the record of God's glory manifested everywhere in nature, and we would not be able to read the Word. Without ears we would not be able to hear the message that God loves us, that He does not hold our sins against us, that He wants to rescue us.

As spectacular as it is, the heart is not much good on its own—all it does is pump insensitive blood. Neither is the impressive brain very functional if not connected to sensory equipment that interfaces with the world and interprets incoming messages. But God is not in the business of neglecting details, so He provided sensory mechanisms so complex and sophisticated that if we had to rent them from an electronics store, we wouldn't be able to afford the price.

The Eye

The eye, claims one influential neo-Darwinian theorist, "is stu-pidly designed."[2] My first reaction upon reading his comment was frank laughter. If the *eye* doesn't impress a biologist, what will it take? The eye is, in fact, an organ of unprecedented sensitivity, precision, complexity, and beauty. If there is no wonder left in your spirit, perhaps the first clue of that lamentable state can be found in a careless disdain for the eye.

Darwin himself did not share the "stupid design" sentiment. "The eye to this day gives me a cold shudder," he confided to a friend. "To suppose that the eye, with all of its inimitable con-trivances for adjusting the focus to different distances, for admitting different amounts of light, and for the correction of spherical and chromatic aberration, could have been formed by natural selection, seems, I freely confess, absurd in the highest pos-sible degree."[3] And this before modern scientific techniques actually revealed the deeper chemical and electrical complexities involved.

First, light encounters the cornea, the primary focusing struc-ture. It then passes through the iris, which controls how much light is allowed to enter. Aside from its ability to constrict or dilate the pupil, the iris also gives the eye its blue-green-brown color. It has 266 identifiable characteristics and is the most data-rich physical structure on the body, far more individual-specific than a fingerprint, which has only about 35 measurable characteristics.[4] One maker of an iris scanner for computer identification purposes claims that the biometric structures of the iris are so unique that there is only a 1 in 10^{78} chance two people's irises will match.[5]

Once through the cornea and iris/pupil, the light passes through the lens for additional focusing. Next stop: the retina, a thin lining in the back of the eye. The retina is comprised of pho-toreceptor cells that are light sensitive, converting the image into electrical signals that can in turn be interpreted by the brain. In contrast to a camera, the eye "takes pictures" continuously and develops them instantaneously—a process we couldn't stop even if we wanted to.

On the retina are 120 million rods and 7 million cones. The

rods accomplish dim vision, night vision, and peripheral vision. The cones are for color vision and fine detail (just remember: *c* is for cones and color). Each eye has one million nerve fibers that electrically connect the photoreceptors in the retina to the visual cortex of the brain. In this center, comprising only 1 percent of the brain cortex, the image is reconstructed in such a way that we "see" it.

Vision functions within a wide spectrum of light availability. The dimmest conditions permitting sight vary from the brightest conditions by a factor of ten billion. Under dim conditions, as in night vision, the rods predominate and life becomes a black-and-white television. Under bright conditions the cones predominate, permitting precise color detail.

The sensitivity of the retina's photoelectric cells is such that as little as 1 to 2 photons of light can trigger a visual signal in each cell. In comparison, a strong flashlight emits 10^{18} photons per second.[6] God, however, does not require photons for His vision, and darkness cannot hide us from His gaze, "for darkness is as light to you."[7] As the psalmist reminds: "He that formed the eye, shall he not see?"[8]

Under very low light conditions it can take the eye sixty minutes to fully accommodate. If the amount of ambient light suddenly decreases, the eye begins a process of adaptation. Within a few minutes, details that at first were not visible begin to clarify. Under conditions of darkness this process of adaptation continues for as long as one hour. If you are star gazing, for example, and wish to observe fine details of the Milky Way, don't turn and glance at a streetlight. Once you do, it will be necessary to begin the low light adaptation process all over again. On the other hand, adaptation to bright light conditions requires a much shorter time frame, usually minutes.

The performance and complexity of the eye are awe-inspiring. Witness the following comparison by a biomedical engineer between the retina and a supercomputer:

> While today's digital hardware is extremely impressive, it is clear that the human retina's real-time performance goes unchallenged. Actually, to simulate 10 milliseconds

of the complete processing of even a single nerve cell from the retina would require the solution of about 500 simultaneous nonlinear differential equations 100 times and would take at least several minutes of processing time on a Cray supercomputer. Keeping in mind that there are 10 million or more such cells interacting with each other in complex ways, it would take a minimum of 100 years of Cray time to simulate what takes place in your eye many times every second.[9]

Other perhaps less impressive but interesting facts about the eye:

- The human eye can distinguish millions of shades of color.
- On a clear dark night we can see a small candle flame from thirty miles away.
- Tears are salty because they are derived from the salt water in the circulatory system.
- Tears are sterile because they contain bacteria-destroying enzymes.
- On average, we blink automatically about every two to ten seconds.
- In a lifetime we blink over 400 million times. (Add one more blink for every time we are photographed.)
- The cornea has extraordinary sensitivity to touch, and anesthesiologists test this corneal reflex to assess depth of anesthesia prior to general surgery.

The eyes are a window to the soul, and a very elegant window at that. By gazing into our eyes other people can discern much about us. There is more involved here than cones, rods, and photons. "Recall the bright, joyful eyes with which your child beams upon you when you bring him a new toy," explains German science writer Gerhard Staguhn, "and then let the physicist tell you that in reality nothing emerges from these eyes: in reality their only objectively detectable function is, continually, to be hit by and to receive light quanta."[10] As Staguhn implies, life is more than physics. We all know it, and God knows it.

We are all born with the same optics but that doesn't mean that we all can "see." Spiritual eyes are an entirely different piece of equipment. When Jesus came and walked among us, some saw Him and some didn't. They all had the same eyes, yet some were spiritually blind, "ever seeing but never perceiving."[11] There is coming a day when all shall be made clear, for at that time "every eye will see him."[12] From my own personal experience, let me assure you that if we have eyes willing to see, God will not hide His glory from us.

The Ear
Just as the eye converts photons into electrical signals that can be "seen" by the brain, so the ear converts sound waves into electrical signals that can be "heard" by the brain—no less a miracle. In some ways the ear actually outperforms the eye. It can hear over an even wider range of sound intensity (one trillion times) than the range of light intensity over which the eye can see (ten billion times).

The eardrum, or tympanic membrane, has the same thickness as a piece of paper and is exquisitely sensitive to any vibration. Even sound waves that move the eardrum less than the diameter of a hydrogen molecule can be perceived by the brain as a sound. It is this sensitivity that makes it possible to hear a cricket chirping one-half mile away on a still night.

The *sensitivity of the hearing mechanism* is very impressive. On the other hand, the *energy of the sound* is distinctly unimpressive. In other words, the reason "sound" happens at all has everything to do with the sensitivity of the equipment God designed for us, and almost nothing to do with the energy of the sound wave itself. A noise loud enough to pain the ear, for example, measures a mere 0.01 watt of energy.[13] The faintest sound audible by the ear has a pressure of 0.0002 dyne per square centimeter—with one dyne being equal to the push of a healthy mosquito.[14]

The sound energy generated by our speaking is likewise negligible. A person could "talk continuously for one hundred years and still not produce the sound energy equivalent to the heat energy needed to bring a cup of water to the boil."[15] (There is always a handful of people, however, who can bring things to a boil with but a few words.) Thus it is the extraordinary sensitivity of the ear itself that permits hearing. The ear, not the sound, deserves all the credit.

The ear has a million moving parts. On the inner surface of the eardrum are attached the tiniest bones in the body: the malleus, incus, and stapes (commonly known as the hammer, anvil, and stirrup). As the eardrum vibrates, the motion is transferred via these three connected bones to the cochlea and the organ of Corti. Within this sensitive tiny organ are thousands of exquisitely sensitive hair cells. The vibration transferred to the hair cells is then converted into an electrical impulse for transmission to the brain via the auditory nerve.

The ear is a microphone, an acoustical amplifier, and a frequency analyzer. It is a musical instrument of sorts: if a piano has eighty-eight keys, the organ of Corti has over twenty thousand keys. It can distinguish between two thousand different pitches. In addition, the ear is a combination range-and-direction finder. First it receives sound data in both sides, and then, by a process called *binaural summation,* it makes lightning-fast calculations to inform the brain of the sound's origin. It can gauge the direction of a sound's origin based on a 0.00003-second difference in its arrival from one ear to the other. And finally, the ear contains a sophisticated balance detection and righting mechanism with over a hundred thousand hair cells functioning as motion sensors.

The ear is yet another evidence of the micro-precision of God. Yet as with so much of life, the creature abuses the gift. The ear is increasingly assaulted by an epidemic of noise and commotion. Noise is to the ear what excessively bright lights are to the eyes. "Noise," wrote Ambrose Bierce, is "a stench in the ear . . . The chief product and authenticating sign of civilization." Leon Trotsky is said to have remarked: "Whoever wishes to live a quiet life should not have been born in the twentieth century."[16]

Noise is not only toxic to the sensitive hair cells of the ear, but it is also damaging to the cardiovascular and nervous systems, as well as to our relationships with God and others. "Noises usually drown out the voice of God," maintains Gordon MacDonald. "Few of us can fully appreciate the terrible conspiracy of noise there is about us, noise that denies us the silence and solitude we need for this cultivation of the inner garden."[17] Dietrich Bonhoeffer concurred. "Regular times of quiet are absolutely necessary. After a time of quiet we meet others in a different and a fresh way," he wrote. "Silence is the simple stillness of the individual under the Word of God."[18]

Considering the developing fetus: by three weeks the ears begin to form; by sixteen weeks babies react to sound; by twenty-eight weeks they register an increased heart rate in response to their mother's voice; and as newborns they are able to recognize their mother when she speaks. A simple question: as His children do we recognize our Father's voice? He gave us ears—do we hear? *Softly and tenderly Jesus is calling . . .*

Smell, Taste, Touch

Mosquitoes can sniff out a human target from as far away as forty miles.[19] Male silkworms can detect females from two miles away. In general, insects and animals are more adept at discerning odors than humans. A dog, for example, has smell-receptor sites that are one hundred times larger than those of humans. A snake can actually "taste" smells. In sticking out its forked tongue, the snake captures odor molecules and brings them into the mouth, where they are identified by the sensitive olfactory organ.

The sense of smell is estimated to be about ten thousand times more sensitive than the sense of taste. When odor chemicals strike the hair cells they trigger a cascade of reactions that convert to electrical signals in the nerve fibers. As little as a single molecule can trigger this reaction. Even though the sense of smell is exquisitely sensitive, it is also easily fatigued. This is why an odor can be highly noticeable at first but later is not sensed at all.

The human nose can distinguish ten thousand different smells.[20] Among the strongest odors we might encounter is mercaptan, an unpleasant-smelling sulfurous substance that can be perceived at the minute concentration of 1 part mercaptan to 460 million parts air.

Taste and smell are closely related senses. If we lose our sense of smell, most of our sense of taste will likewise disappear. Humans have nine thousand taste buds in the mouth, and their sensitivity is sufficient to taste 0.04 ounce of table salt dissolved in 530 quarts of water.

The sense of touch incorporates many distinct elements: pressure, pain, heat, cold, and touch. The body has 450 touch cells per square inch of skin. We can detect a smooth plane of glass from one etched with lines only 1/2500th of an inch deep.[21] We can "feel" a pressure on our fingertips or face that depresses the skin a microscopic 0.00004 inch. We can tell the difference between a letter weighing 1¼ ounces and one weighing 1½ ounces, but not between 10 pounds and 10¼ pounds—the difference needs to be at least 2 percent.

The Scriptures are full of references to these senses brought into the spiritual realm. We are to be a sweet fragrance;[22] to taste that the LORD is good;[23] to touch no unclean thing.[24] In the manifestation of each sense are two potent reminders: first, that God is an aesthetic genius; and second, that all His gifts are for the purposes of His glory, never to be abused.

CHAPTER FOUR

The BRAIN *and* NERVOUS SYSTEM

"IN man is a three-pound brain, which, as far as we know, is the most complex and orderly arrangement of matter in the universe." Thus wrote scientist and author Isaac Asimov.[1] In so stating, it appears to me that he was giving God a compliment, even though he remained an avowed atheist until his death in 1992.

The brain—pride and joy of the nervous system—is staggering in its abilities and complexity. Despite all of our modern scientific research, we are only beginning to penetrate the brain's secrets.

The basic cell of the brain is called the *neuron*, of which there are ten billion (some estimate as high as 100 billion). This seems like a large number, but it requires only thirty-three doublings of the first neuron cell to arrive at the ten billion.[2] In addition to long extensions called *axons*, each neuron has ten thousand tiny branching fibers and filamentous projections called *dendrites*, a name derived from the Greek word for *tree*. Each neuron is thus in contact with ten thousand other neurons, for a total of 100 trillion neurological interconnections.

If you were to stretch out all the neurons and dendritic connections in the brain and lay them end to end, they would reach for 100 thousand miles and circle the earth at the equator four times. (That's why it takes two Valium.) One way to visualize these dendritic connections is as light switches, in either the *off* or *on* position. The brain holds 10^{14} bits of information and thus has a storage capacity one thousand times that of a Cray-2 supercomputer.[3]

The capacity of the brain is such that it can hold information equivalent to that contained in twenty-five million books, enough to fill a bookshelf 500 miles long. In contrast, the Library of Congress has seventeen million volumes. The deoxyribonucleic acid (DNA)-based human genome is spectacular in its own right, as we shall see in the next chapter. But the human brain has ten thousand times the capacity for storing information as the human genome.[4]

Assuming that 10 percent of the brain cells are firing at any given time, this implies a rate of a thousand trillion computations per second. It makes you wonder why balancing the checkbook is so hard.

Unlike the parts of a computer, nerve cells are highly individual. No two cells are exactly the same, nor do they respond to the same incoming information in the same way. Each neuron is unique in all the universe. God, it seems to me, really outdid Himself.

Even though the brain triples in size from birth to adulthood, we do not add any new neurons. The orthodox position for decades has been that neurons don't replace themselves and don't regenerate. They are capable of living for a hundred years, but when they die, they die. When it happens, we have no choice but to subtract one from the IQ column. Now, however, new research indicates that neuronal regeneration does indeed happen, and perhaps commonly.[5] Still, the clinical fact remains—neurological disease and injury are almost always tragically permanent and irreversible.

Neurotransmitters

Neurons work by a combination of electrical and chemical signals. Within the neuron itself the signal is electrical. But where one nerve connects with its neighbor, in a connection called a *synapse,* the signal switches into a chemical message. This chemical signal must be ferried across the synapse by a neurotransmitter. There are more than one hundred different neurotransmitters, including such headline grabbers as serotonin and dopamine.

Imagine it like this: we travel down the road at 400 mph in a supercharged electric car—no exhaust, no noise, just speed. When we come to a river, however, we stop the car, load it on the ferry, dawdle across the river, unload the car—and then resume our furious dash down the road. In much the same way, the speed of electrical conduction down the nerve is rapid (maximum speed actually is 400 mph), but the chemical transport at the synapse is much slower—rather like waiting for a web page to download. It is not slow by normal human standards, for it happens in a few thousandths of a second. But in terms of the nervous system, that's like waiting for a glacier to move.

A great deal of current brain research is being conducted in this area of neurotransmitters. With a newer and clearer understanding comes the hope for precise medications targeted to specific neurological dysfunction. I suffer from migraine headaches, for example, and some of the new neurotransmitter-based medicines have been of great benefit in arresting such headaches while still in the early stages.

Brain Waves, Prayer, and God's ESP

The electrical activity of the brain not only generates current running down the neurons, but also is responsible for brain waves. A tracing of brain waves, called the electroencephalogram (EEG), is obtained by placing electrodes on various portions of the scalp and recording what comes through from the brain. (Never mind that a playful professor once hooked up a bowl of Jell-O to an EEG machine and obtained a readout that was "virtually identical to the brain waves of healthy humans."[6] That, as far as I am concerned, is just more evidence of God's sense of humor.)

There are four basic types of waves obtained by the EEG recorder:

alpha waves	→	relaxed but aware
beta waves	→	fully alert
delta waves	→	sleeping
theta waves	→	drowsy

A recent development in the application of brain waves is provocative in both its medical and theological implications. Work is now being done in patients who have paralyzing illnesses, such as amyotrophic lateral sclerosis (ALS, also known as Lou Gehrig's disease). In advanced stages this disease leaves the body completely paralyzed but permits otherwise normal brain functioning. (The noted British physicist Stephen Hawking has ALS, although a more slowly progressing variety than usual.)

It has now been demonstrated that ALS patients, with electrodes on their scalp, can control a computer screen by manipulating brain waves called *slow cortical potentials*.[7] Using a "thought translation device," these patients can "amplify and dampen their brain waves in a way that allows them to select letters on a video screen and spell out messages."[8] "For the first time," says one of the researchers, "we have shown that it is possible to communicate with nothing but one's own brain and to escape, at least verbally, the locked-in state."[9]

This provides exciting possibilities for fully paralyzed people—even those with feeding tubes and respirators—not only to spell out letters on the computer screen, but also to turn on and off the lights, run electronic equipment, and even "think" directions to their own wheelchairs. Taking it one step further, the possibility exists of going wireless: "If the electronics are sensitive enough, they might be able to grab brain waves out of the air."[10]

What "theological implications" might this have? I occasionally wonder how God reads thoughts. I'm sure most believing Christians have never concerned themselves with such a question but instead simply accept by faith that a sovereign God can do anything He wants, including getting inside our brains and easily reading our minds. "You perceive my thoughts from afar," wrote David in a much-loved psalm. "Before a word is on my tongue you know it completely, O LORD."[11] Most of our prayer life, specifically silent prayer, functions precisely along the lines of such orthodoxy. And I am not sure that we need to do anything more theologically than to leave it right there.

Still, at other times we act as if we naïvely assume our thoughts are private and thus exempt from God's monitoring. I don't believe it for a minute. If we speak words, He hears. If we merely think silent thoughts, He hears just as clearly. We can't hide inside our craniums, so it is no use pretending about it.

I have never personally stumbled over this issue of God's ESP, nor entertained doubts. But I have from time to time wondered, "How does He do it?" Now we have perhaps the beginnings of a mechanism in biophysics that explains one possible scenario that God could use, should He choose to do so. (And this is not to say that God in fact *needs* such a mechanism.) If in the process of "thinking," we generate electrical signals, and if in some general form these electrical signals can penetrate the skull and be picked up on the scalp and even in the air beyond the scalp, then it is certainly possible for God to intercept such thoughts at any point in the process.

If you think this is a superfluous science fiction discussion, then for you it is. But if you are among those who are both skeptical and cynical about how God performs such ESP, understand that there is an increasing foundation in biophysics behind God's claim for sovereignty in the realm of continuously discerning our thoughts.

There is one additional aspect of prayer that mystifies some people and that perhaps we can touch on before leaving the subject: How can God hear a billion people pray at the same time? C. S. Lewis dealt with this precise issue:

> A man can put it to me by saying "I can believe in God all right, but what I cannot swallow is the idea of Him attending to several hundred million human beings who are all addressing Him at the same moment." . . . The whole sting of it comes in the words *at the same moment*. Most of us can imagine God attending to any number of applicants if only they came one by one and He had an endless time to do it in.
>
> Almost certainly God is not in Time. His life does not consist of moments following one another. If a million people are praying to Him at ten-thirty tonight, He need not listen to them all in that one little snippet which we call ten-thirty. Ten-thirty — and every other

moment from the beginning of the world—is always the Present for Him. If you like to put it that way, He has all eternity in which to listen to the split second of prayer put up by a pilot as his plane crashes in flames.[12]

There is abundant reason in the study of contemporary physics for us to view God as having "all the time in the world" to do whatever it is He wishes to do—and that includes listening to and answering our prayers. And there is new evidence in modern biophysics to suggest a mechanism whereby God can actually read our thoughts (again, this is not to say that He requires such a device). The conclusion: if we have a problem believing any of the specifics of how prayer works, the problem is ours and not God's.

Memory
Even though we know that the brain generates both electrical and chemical activity, we still do not know precisely what thinking is, or intuition, or consciousness, or what distinguishes the mind from the brain. Some believe it is only a matter of additional research before all becomes clear. Others disagree. To them, the brain is a black box that will always be more than the sum of its parts.

For example, how did Einstein's brain do it? In 1905, he was poor, underemployed, estranged from the world, rejected by Europe's academic establishment, without a country, and stung by his parents' disdain for his older Serbian wife. Yet somehow in that "one miraculous year," at the age of twenty-six he published five papers that changed our fundamental understanding of physics forever. Any one of these papers, dealing with such topics as time, space, light, energy, speed, relativity, and $E = mc^2$, would have secured his place in history. One paper won him the Nobel Prize. How does a brain overturn firmly entrenched paradigms with impossibly complex levels of abstract thought that have nothing to do with measurable day-to-day experience? "The level of genius," wrote one observer, "is practically incomprehensible."[13]

Other stunning mental accomplishments come from the

experience of autistic savants. These are people with severe mental handicaps juxtaposed with prodigious mental abilities, usually in the area of mathematics, memory, art, or music. They have "the puzzling paradox of being backward and brilliant at the same time," explains savant authority Darold A. Treffert, M.D.[14] Savants reveal phenomenal abilities of a special type—very narrow but exceedingly deep, sometimes called "islands of intelligence." Take, for example, the following cases:

> George and Charles, identical twins, are calendar calculators. Give them a date and they can give you the day of the week over a span of eighty thousand years—forty thousand backward or forty thousand forward. Ask them to name in which years of the next 200 (or any 200) Easter will fall on March 23 and they will name those years with lightning rapidity. They cannot count to thirty, but they swap twenty-digit prime numbers for amusement.
>
> Leslie is blind, is severely mentally handicapped, has cerebral palsy, and has never had any formal musical training. Yet, in his teens, upon hearing Tchaikovsky's Piano Concerto No. 1 for the first time, he played it back on the piano flawlessly and without hesitation.
>
> Jedediah has a mental age of ten and is unable to write his name. When asked the question: "In a body whose three sides are 23,145,789 yards, 5,642,732 yards, and 54,965 yards, how many cubicle ⅛ths of an inch exist?" he provided the correct twenty-eight-digit figure after a five-hour computation. "Would you like the answer backwards or forwards?"[15]

What does this tell us about the inherent capacity of the human brain—about how it learns, how it calculates, how it performs? What does this tell us about the Mind of God, who designed and wired such a brain?

One Indian student memorized the non-repeating number Pi to the thirty-thousandth digit, only to be outdone by a Japanese man who remembered it to forty-two thousand digits. One

German musician read an unfamiliar symphony only once before conducting it from memory later that evening. An Edinburgh mathematician was asked to divide four by forty-seven. After slightly more than half a minute of giving numbers, and having reached forty-six decimal places, he said he "had arrived at the repeating point." Wolfgang Mozart reported that "an entire new composition" would suddenly arise in his head.[16] What do such prodigious feats reveal about the brain's inherent capacity? How will this brain perform when fallenness is removed and it assumes its glorified and fully redeemed state?

The study of how memory works is still progressing, but some factors have been clarified:

- Memory is not necessarily a function of *study* or *time*.
- *Short-term* memory and *long-term* memory are two different commodities.
- Emotional states and moods can greatly affect memory.
- *Visual images* and *linguistic memories* are stored differently.
- Learning and memory are highly individual experiences.
- Forgetting is as important as remembering.

Memory is not necessarily a function of study *or* time.

The amount of effort we put into learning is not necessarily the most important thing. It turns out that *meaning* is as important to memory as *intention*. In other words, just because we open up a history book does not mean we will remember history. "Remembering does not happen as a matter of course whenever a person is exposed to information," states education and information expert Jeremy Campbell. "It does not even happen automatically if the person wants and intends to commit the information to memory. . . . Questions such as how long a time was spent in trying to store it in memory are of surprisingly little importance." Campbell summarizes by stating: "Clearly, meaning is an important ingredient in remembering."[17]

Short-term *memory and* long-term *memory are two different commodities.*

These two types of memory are apparently located in different places in the brain and etched there by different mechanisms. Short-term memory is held for only a matter of minutes and can be maddenly unreliable. (Where did I put those keys?) "You are more likely to remember your childhood," observed Bill Cosby, "than the place you left your glasses."[18] It is the short-term memory that is most affected by aging and illness. Long-term memory, however, seems to result in a "memory trace," a molecular and cellular alteration, being etched in the brain structure. Long-term memories can often be recalled by people with perfect clarity, even decades later.

Emotional states and moods can greatly affect memory.

Something that was joyous or tragic seems to etch itself more clearly in the brain. If you were at a Chicago Bulls championship game, you will most likely remember what the weather was like. And among those of us who were alive then, who doesn't remember what he or she was doing when JFK was shot?

Visual images *and* linguistic memories *are stored differently.*

When we *hear* something, the memory goes down one pathway and is stored in a certain way. When we *see* something, the brain uses a different pathway and different storage venue. Visual images can be powerful triggers for remembering. It has been asserted that by the time we are thirty, each of us carries around with us a mental videotape cassette containing some three trillion pictures and holograms of ourselves in action.[19] These pictures are indelibly imprinted, which is one reason R-rated movies are worrisome. Once those images are stored in the film archives of our brains, there is no delete button.

Not only is the visual versus linguistic distinction important in memory, but it apparently is true even in the initiation and conceptualization of thought. "Contemporary authorities agree that the form a thought takes in our minds is usually verbal, but not necessarily so," explains creative thinking authority Vincent Ryan Ruggiero. "Just as we may *express* an idea in mathematical symbols or pictures, in addition to words, we may also *conceive* of it that way."[20] At age thirteen, for example, Einstein envisioned himself riding on a beam of light. His visual imagination thus helped him transcend fixed bounds and creatively explore a new and counterintuitive realm.

Learning and memory are highly individual experiences.

People have different learning styles. Some need a quiet atmosphere and clear desk. Others prefer to be plugged into loud music and sit in the midst of an open-book and scattered-paper uproar. In medicine, some physicians learn well by reading case histories. Most, however, learn best when immersed in the clinical context. In my own situation, reading about a disease in a book yielded a relatively low learning efficiency. Once I saw the disease in the context of a patient experience, however, I would never forget it. "If memory is to work well, the rememberer must pick up those aspects of the events or material to be remembered that make possible a well-defined personal experience. . . . It is the quality of the experience that counts, and that is never quite the same for each person," explains Campbell. "The brain constructs and reconstructs information, creating a highly personal mental artifact and calling it a memory. . . . Each act of memory must be special, even unique, to each person."[21]

Forgetting is as important as remembering.

As important as memory is for our day-to-day functioning, selective and appropriate forgetting is likewise important for our day-to-day emotional health. Unfortunately, we have no volitional control over forgetting. Every day our brains absorb large quantities of useless or harmful debris. Much of it lodges within our memory banks even though we have no desire to remember it and no functional need to recall it. When the ancient Greek Simonides offered to teach Themistocles the art of memory, he refused. "Teach me not the art of remembering," he said, "but the art of forgetting, for I remember things I do not wish to remember, but I cannot forget things I wish to forget."²²

"In the practical use of our intellect, forgetting is as important a function as remembering," said William James. "If we remembered everything, we should on most occasions be as ill off as if we remembered nothing."²³ Forgetting, for example, is an important component of forgiveness. If someone has offended us, do we forgive and forget? Love, the Scriptures teach, "keeps no record of wrongs."²⁴

God, it seems, preserves for Himself the right and ability to forget. "I will forgive their wickedness," He said, "and will remember their sins no more."²⁵ Would that we had such an ability, or that we even had the inclination toward such an ability. "A good memory is fine," someone once said, "but the ability to forget is the true test of greatness." And of godliness.

We should not leave a discussion of this remarkable human capacity for memory without mentioning God's explicit and frequent command "to remember." He gave us the gift of memory for many reasons, but chief among them is so that we might remember Him and His great deeds on our behalf.

For example, the recounting of the Ten Commandments in Deuteronomy 5 explains that the Sabbath is set aside, in part, to remember: "Remember that you were slaves in Egypt and that the LORD your God brought you out of there with a mighty hand and an outstretched arm. Therefore the LORD your God has commanded you to observe the Sabbath day."²⁶

Just three chapters later, in five separate verses, Moses again exhorts the people of Israel to remember:

- "Remember how the LORD your God led you all the way in the desert these forty years" (8:2).
- "Be careful that you do not forget the LORD your God, failing to observe his commands" (8:11).
- Otherwise, when you have fine houses, large herds, and much silver and gold, "your heart will become proud and you will forget the LORD your God, who brought you out of Egypt" (8:14).

- "Remember the LORD your God, for it is he who gives you the ability to produce wealth" (8:18).
- "If you ever forget the LORD your God and follow other gods and worship and bow down to them, I testify against you today that you will surely be destroyed" (8:19).

Such memory is the source of gratitude and the guarantor of righteous behavior. On the other hand, such forgetting is the source of much misery.

If God created within us a remarkable brain and granted us the gift of memory so that we might bind ourselves in remembrance to Him, how great the injustice when we turn that capacity against Him in haughty arrogance. Instead, we ought to carefully use our memory for purposes of righteousness. "Look to the LORD and his strength; seek his face always," wrote the psalmist. "Remember the wonders he has done, his miracles."[27]

Language

Another remarkable function of the brain is language acquisition. This includes both the learning of language and the use of language as a social tool. The process begins very early. Although not intelligibly, babies babble and coo. Within a period of months, however, they intuitively begin to realize that the strange noises made by people around them are not babble at all but sounds connected to meaning. Once this understanding develops, babies begin a rapid acquisition of the language capacity.

By one year of age, infants are using one or more words with meaning. By eighteen months, their vocabulary consists of 20 words, and one-fourth of their speech is intelligible. By two years, their vocabulary grows to 300 words, and two-thirds of what they say is intelligible. By three years, the vocabulary has ballooned to 1,000 words, 90 percent of which are intelligible. By the time they enter school, the vocabulary has risen to 3,000 to 4,000 words. This trajectory of language and vocabulary acquisition continues in an upward climb (except perhaps for the adolescent years, when vocabulary regresses back to a few words such as "boring" and "whatever"). The average adult has an *active* or *use* vocabulary of 10,000 words and a *passive* or *recognition* vocabulary of 30,000 to 40,000 words. For comparison, *Webster's New International Dictionary* defines 400,000 words, and the English language probably contains one million words—no one knows the exact number.

No other animal has the kind of language capacity God provides humans. Other animals share with us the abilities of walking, running, seeing, hearing, and smelling. But the gift of language is reserved for humans. Why did He single us out in this way? He could have created us without ears or vocal cords and forced us to depend on more primitive mechanisms for communication. If He had done so, I can guarantee none of us today would be postulating that God forgot something. If hearing, ears, and vocal cords did not exist and someone imaginatively postulated what it would be like to have this thing called language, that person would be laughed into submission, lumped into the same category as flakes who believe in UFOs.

But the fact remains, God *did* give us such equipment, and, I believe, for a specific reason—relationship, communication, and love. God is pro-relationship. It is on His heart constantly.

We spend ten to twelve cumulative years of our lives talking. And of course this talking is in the context of other people. Helen Keller maintained that the gift of hearing was far more important than the gift of sight—because hearing allows the gift of speech, and speech allows the nurturing of relationship. Language connects us to the hearts of others in a way that nothing else can.

The brain is capable of thinking at a rate of 800 words per minute,[28] far exceeding the speed of caution. (As someone once warned: Be careful of your thoughts, for they might break into words at any moment.) When thinking is transferred into language, you automatically and simultaneously manage to "monitor your muscles, order your syntax, watch out for semantic catastrophes that would result from a slight change in word order, continuously adjust your tone of voice and expressive gestures, and say something meaningful when it would have been so easy to speak gibberish."[29] Language seems easy; it most definitely is not.

On the receptive side, the brain has recently been shown to have the amazing capacity to even understand speech that has been intentionally garbled. "Humans' ability to understand speech is so deeply ingrained that people can even decipher sentences that have been recorded, chopped up into brief segments and played backwards," explains Dr. Joseph M. Mercola.

> Researchers sliced digitally recorded sentences into very short segments, reversed each snippet while leaving it in its proper place in the sentence, then played the distorted speech to seven test subjects. The participants had no problem understanding the sentences. Their brains were apparently able to perceive the syllables as sounding nearly the same whether heard backwards or forwards.
>
> The research demonstrates that many areas of the brain are used to handle complicated auditory signals. . . . Anyone who has gone to a party held in a crowded room filled with music and chattering people has tapped those skills to understand what others are saying. What this tells us is that speech is quite robust. We can perceive it even when a number of things have been done to distort or muddy the signal. Somehow the information is preserved or at least recoverable to us even when it's played backwards.[30]

Yet as with all of God's gifts, the gift of language can be corrupted. The same language ability that can be endearing and winsome is often instead used to condemn, control, gossip, and curse. "With the tongue we praise our Lord and Father," explained James, "and with it we curse men, who have been made in God's likeness."[31]

Using language for the building of relationships is primarily helpful on the horizontal, earthly plane—we do not necessarily require the gift of language for divine communication. The language of heaven is surely more than words. It is not words, it is meaning. Those who worship Him must worship Him in Spirit and truth. We must communicate more than just words if we are to worship God, or our language will not survive the great device at the entrance of heaven that filters out emptiness. Our words are simply vessels for us to use, vessels that in themselves are empty. If we don't fill the word vessels with true worship and prayer, they will never take wing to the Father's ears.

Never let us think that we accomplished anything on a Sunday morning because we met and exchanged an hour's worth of words. But rather let us consider this—did we use all our heart to fill those words with our thanksgiving and adoration? As the hymn says: "What language shall I borrow to thank thee, dearest Friend?"

Sleep

Sleep is yet another poorly understood human activity under the control of the remarkable brain. God could have created us without the need for sleep, but He didn't. Fish don't sleep—they don't have eyelids. They just go to the bottom of the lake and stare at a rock all night. Giraffes sleep about ten minutes a day. Dolphins sleep with just half of their brain at a time so the other half can keep them swimming. Cows get three hours of sleep every twenty-four hours. God could have created us with negligible sleep needs, but for reasons only He fully knows, that would not have suited His deeper purposes.

Throughout the duration of our lives we will sleep a total of twenty-four years, one-third of our time on planet earth. Newborns require sixteen hours of sleep a day. That amount gradually tapers down to seven to eight hours during our adult and senior years. The optimal duration of sleep per night varies from person to person, but in general it is the amount of sleep that permits a person to feel wide awake and alert throughout the day.

In absence of light cues, humans tend to choose a long sleep-wake day of about twenty-five hours.[32] In other words, if placed in a cave with no external signals, most of us would assume a sleep-wake cycle that is longer than the twenty-four-hour day our spinning earth gives us. Theologically, I have absolutely no idea why this should be so.

This leads to the somewhat related and often misunderstood

issue of night owls versus early birds. It is important to understand that there are legitimate physiologic differences between the two. Without a gracious understanding of these differences we tend to unnecessarily criticize one another. The early bird thinks the night owl is lazy for not rising to meet the dawn, while the night owl thinks the early bird has no stamina for late night work. Personally, my productivity is greatly enhanced in the evening and even late night. Ninety percent of my writing occurs between 10:00 P.M. and 7:00 A.M. If I were to switch styles and get up early to write, it would be a complete waste of time.

There are two types of sleep: rapid eye movement (REM) and non-REM. The non-REM sleep is further subdivided into four stages. Stage 1 sleep is *twilighting*, when we first drift across that magic line that divides wakefulness and sleep. If someone comes into the room when we are in Stage 1, he or she is likely to apologize for waking us, only to have us reply: "Oh, you didn't wake me . . . I don't think . . . what time is it anyway? Why is my book on the floor?" At the other end of the sleep spectrum is Stage 4, the deepest level, where we drool on ourselves. It is interesting to note that sleep is a dynamic event. Throughout the night we are drifting up and down through these various levels of sleep (oftentimes even rising to momentary wakefulness that we later do not remember) and also in and out of REM.

REM sleep is the domain of dreams. We spend 25 to 35 percent of our sleep budget in REM. Some have called REM a third state of consciousness, different from either wakefulness or non-REM sleep. While in REM, our mind is hyperalert but our muscles are paralyzed. A good thing, too, otherwise our dreams would have us running all over the neighborhood.

REM seems to serve the purpose of helping people organize their thoughts during sleep. Problems are often solved during REM; who hasn't said, "Let me sleep on it"? Creativity is nourished. Perhaps that is why Einstein routinely got eleven hours of sleep a night. In addition, I believe God often speaks to us during sleep. "I will praise the LORD, who counsels me," wrote David. "Even at night my heart instructs me."[33] In addition, many times in the Scriptures God appeared to people in a dream. Even if we don't completely understand the role of dreams, God has a purpose in using them.

If people try to interfere with God's natural plan for sleep, dysfunction follows. It is an experiment our entire nation has decided to pursue. In 1850 the average amount of sleep was nine and a half hours per night. By 1910, it was nine hours per night. By 1950, it was eight hours per night. And by 1990, the average amount of sleep per night was down to seven hours. In other words, the average American today gets two and a half fewer hours of sleep than 150 years ago. One-third of us sleep fewer than six hours per night during workdays, and fifty to seventy million Americans have sleep disorders. A staggering 27 percent of the general population admitted to falling asleep while driving in the last year.[34]

The longest recorded continuous period of wakefulness was 264 hours, accomplished in 1965 by a high school student named Randy Gardner who went without sleep for a science project.[35] Personally, I can think of easier ways to get an "A." Just reading about this science experiment makes me tired, and brings to mind the W. C. Fields comment, "The best cure for insomnia is to get a lot of sleep."

There is a reason God created sleep. Scripture teaches us that God grants sleep to those He loves.[36] If we insist on calling sleep a waste of time, we will have to take it up with the Creator Himself.

Perhaps part of His reason for creating sleep is to teach us to trust His sovereignty. It takes an act of faith to quit at the end of a day without all our problems solved, our to-do list completed, or the world fixed. At that point, we must trust God to run the universe without our help. A daily reminder of Who is in charge.

The Brain and the Soul Catcher

The brain is so complex, wrote evolutionist Michael Denton in 1985, that even using the most sophisticated engineering techniques it "would take an eternity" for engineers to assemble an object remotely resembling it.[37] Yet today British Telecommunications researchers are attempting to do precisely that. Engineers are building the Soul Catcher, a computer system designed to capture the nervous system's electrical activity, which would preserve our thoughts and emotions.

The hardware for early versions of "virtual immortality" already exists. Tiny video cameras embedded in eyeglass frames document every activity of daily living and feed it into a hard disk worn in a pendant. But the Soul Catcher would eventually use a wearable supercomputer, perhaps in a wristwatch, with wireless links to microsensors under the scalp and in the nerves that carry all five sensory signals. At that point wearing a video camera would no longer be required.

Eventually, these efforts will coalesce into "organized, online archives of everything that happens," predicts D. Raj Reddy, a professor of computer science at Carnegie Mellon University. These signals could be preserved for the day when they can be transferred to silicon circuits to rejuvenate minds as immortal entities. "Researchers can only wonder what it will be like," wrote Otis Port in *Business Week*, "to wake up one day and find yourself alive inside a machine."[38] Personally, I can envision a somewhat better and certainly more straightforward way to achieve immortality.

When God designed the brain, He became the original computer scientist. He built a unit of remarkable sophistication, complexity, and beauty. Despite the fact that the entire brain creates only about twenty watts of power, its performance is astounding. The brain's curriculum vitae, according to brain expert Todd Siler, reveals it to function in more than 200 ways: alignment equipment, altitude and heading reference systems, data processing equipment, direction finders, closed-circuit television displays, distance measuring equipment, optical guidance systems, information retrieval systems, night vision equipment, noise measurement equipment, recording equipment, strategic acquisition and direction-finding systems, frequency synthesizers, velocity-measuring equipment, and so forth.[39]

It would appear to me that with an entry like the brain, God would be in the finalist competition for the Westinghouse Science Award.

The Brain and Truth
Any discussion of the brain in the context of faith would be incomplete if it did not at least attempt to clarify the limits of what the

brain can do, that is, the spiritual limits of knowledge. The brain is a proven expert in the gathering and processing of data and information. But can we trust it to bring us all the way Home? Sadly, we cannot.

There is no clear correlation between filling the mind with facts and discovering Truth; between advancing in educational attainment and advancing in the things of God; between IQ and righteousness. Should we then forsake education and go in the other direction? On the contrary, we *should* instruct and discipline the brain. But if at the beginning of every day the brain will not humbly bow to Truth, then our synapses are pointed in the wrong direction. Paul, one of history's most brilliant thinkers, warned: "We demolish arguments and every pretension that sets itself up against the knowledge of God, and we take captive every thought to make it obedient to Christ."[40]

The brain is the realm of data, information, and knowledge. The spirit, however, is the realm of understanding, wisdom, and Truth. The brain and the spirit need to register for classes together in the halls of education, and their togetherness needs to be fixed. Harvard University, for example, had in its original charter this statement: "Let every student well consider . . . that the main end of his life and studies is to know God and Jesus Christ."[41] Somewhere in the process of gaining prestige they lost Eternity. And such a loss can never be compensated by piling up Nobel laureates, for it is written, "I will destroy the wisdom of the wise; the intelligence of the intelligent I will frustrate."[42]

The brain must act humbly or it will sabotage its own search. God resists the proud, and He surely and reliably will resist the brain when it defies Him. This is why, sadly, many brilliant thinkers stumble in the darkness their entire lives. As A. W. Tozer accurately warned: "The uncomprehending mind is unaffected by truth."[43] God has ordained from the beginning that worldly learning will never be sufficient to reveal Christ.[44] This does not, of course, mean that the message of Christ is irrational, but only that it is extra-rational. Its meaning is not accessible through neurons and synapses, no matter how exceptional. To see Christ requires that a light be turned on in our understanding, and the light switch is controlled by God and not by the brain. This has upset many prominent scholars throughout the ages, but it is a matter God alone adjudicates and so far He has not changed His ruling in the matter.

God's published opinion on knowledge, wisdom, understanding, and truth:

- "The fear of the LORD is the beginning of wisdom."[45]
- "Has not God made foolish the wisdom of the world?"[46]
- "Your wisdom and knowledge mislead you when you say to yourself, 'I am, and there is none besides me.'"[47]
- "If I have . . . all knowledge . . . but have not love, I am nothing."[48]
- "There will be terrible times in the last days. People will be . . . always learning but never able to acknowledge the truth."[49]
- "Sanctify them by the truth; your word is truth."[50]
- "That the God of our Lord Jesus Christ, the Father of glory, may give unto you the spirit of wisdom and revelation in the knowledge of him: The eyes of your understanding being enlightened."[51]

"Knowledge puffs up," explained Paul.[52] Following two millennia of progress, the puff factor has now grown quite pompous. Francis Bacon said knowledge is power, and in today's economy indeed it is. But knowledge is insufficient. T. S. Eliot in *The Rock* bemoaned the loss of transcendence:

Where is the Life we have lost in living?
Where is the wisdom we have lost in knowledge?
Where is the knowledge we have lost in information?[53]

The British scholar Paul Johnson, in researching a scathing book about the personal lives of intellectuals, came to the following stern conclusion:

Intellectuals have the arrogance to believe that they can use their brains to tell humanity how to conduct its affairs. In so doing, they turn their backs on natural law, inherited wisdom and the religious background that have traditionally defined the aims of society. They find it hard to admit that there is a higher authority than their own judgment; they have a deep-rooted and tremendously powerful arrogance.

An intellectual consensus can and often does become a general consensus, warned Johnson, because intellectuals "are very influential, powerful people who have a gift for words and access to the media. That's why I think they are so dangerous. . . . One should listen to and read intellectuals but not necessarily take great notice of what they say, particularly when they gang up and produce manifestoes."[54]

World-class brain researcher Sir John Eccles, himself a Nobel laureate in medicine and physiology and a Christian, offers this perspective:

We need to discredit the belief held by many scientists that science will ultimately deliver the final truth. . . . Unfortunately, many scientists and interpreters of science don't understand the limits of the discipline. They claim much more for it than they should. They argue that someday science will explain values, beauty, love, friendship, aesthetics and literary quality. They say: "All of these will eventually be explicable in terms of brain performance. We only have to know more about the brain." That view is nothing more than a superstition that confuses both the public and many scientists.[55]

Quite honestly, if we wish to be straight about it, the brain is having trouble even understanding *itself*, let alone God. When someone challenged Woody Allen to explain God, he quipped, "I can't explain God to you. I don't even know how my toaster works." Author Lyall Watson drives perhaps the final nail in the coffin of neuronal presumption: "If the brain were so simple that we could understand it, we would be so simple that we couldn't understand it."[56]

The brain is quite spectacular in its own right, and it does not need inflated claims about its potential. Let's challenge it diligently to learn, but then let's accept the borders it cannot cross. Even given its limitations, the brain's amazing capacity speaks to the genius of the God who endowed it.

CHAPTER FIVE

The CELL, GENES, and DNA

E VEN though we have already briefly examined the world of the cell, let's revisit that terrain to get a glimpse of perhaps the most spectacular of all human miracles—the DNA. If for some reason you are still a skeptic needing more evidence of the genius and majesty of God, you will perhaps find it here.

The cell, composed predominantly of carbon-based ingredients, is the basic structure of living matter. An adult human body contains tens of trillions of cells.[1] Because trillions of these cells die every day, the body always has a repair kit on hand to make duplicate copies as rapidly as the old cells disappear.

Each individual cell floats in a swimming pool called the *interstitial fluid*. This fluid is rich with molecules that have just come from the bloodstream and are now dog-paddling their way over to the cell. Once they arrive at the cell door, they knock at the tiny pore openings in the cell membrane and request permission to enter. If the cell has need of their services, molecules such as oxygen, glucose, and small proteins are invited in.

Once inside, these newly arriving molecules probably gasp in astonishment. The cell's interior must feel like a combination video arcade and Radio City Music Hall. Things are popping everywhere, for they have entered a protoplasmic pyrotechnic factory in hyperdrive. In fact, it is a shrine to God's efficiency and precision. He probably visits it now and then, lingering in the lobby just to enjoy that which He has made.

The cell itself is intricate and complex, made up of many tiny specialized structures. The membrane is a microscopic miracle all its own, functioning crucially in the exchange of important materials. Electrical forces (each cell has an electrical potential difference across the cell membrane) play an important role in cellular functioning, with perhaps a lightning strike from time to time to keep the mitochondria entertained. Speaking of the mitochondria, they are the tiny engines of each cell busily making the fuel ATP. Food is oxidized within the cells. Carbon dioxide and other waste products are dispatched to the lungs or kidneys, no doubt waving good-bye as they pass the inbound oxygen and nutrients. Then there are the lysosomes, the endoplasmic reticulum, the Golgi apparatus, the ribosomes, and more—but you don't have to worry about these structures other than to realize that the cell is a very active, crowded place.

Also buried deep in each cell is the nucleus. This is the epicenter of the cell's functioning. If the mitochondrion is the *heart* of the cell and the membrane is the *skin* of the cell, then the nucleus is the *brain* of the cell. The nucleus contains twenty-three pairs of chromosomes, and here is where the story becomes interesting. But we are getting ahead of ourselves. Let's rewind the video camera all the way back to the beginning . . .

The First Cell
All of these tens of trillions of cells began very inauspiciously as one single, tiny, minuscule, microscopic, almost invisible speck—the fertilized egg. This cell is the result of the union of the male sperm and female egg (as if I have to explain that to you). The sperm is among the smallest cells in the body, while the egg is among the largest cells and, in addition, contributes essentially all of the energy-producing mitochondria.[2] I told you God has a sense of humor. But before males get too depressed by it all, just remember that you beat out 200 million other sperm to get where you are today—no small feat.

Within this tiny first cell, measuring mere microns, is the

blueprint for building an entire human body with a complexity that is incomprehensible. Think about it. Let's do a comparison: I am a grown adult with a sophisticated education including degrees in both medicine and physics—but I can't even figure out how to set the clock on my car radio. On the other hand, here is a single fertilized ovum, smaller than the period at the end of this sentence, that with apparent ease directs the proliferation and differentiation of tens of trillions of cells, as various from each other as the retina is from the toenail. As I said, think about it.

Thirty hours after fertilization, en route down the Fallopian tubes and headed for the uterus, this single precocious cell undergoes its first division. The resultant twin cells, still bonded tightly together, continue to divide at a faster rate, roughly twice a day. Doing the math of exponential growth, we notice that it doesn't take long for the two cells to become two thousand, two million, and then two billion.

Sometime within the first couple of weeks, in addition to dividing, the cells also begin to *differentiate*. Even though we start out with cells that look identical, after the process of differentiation one cell goes off in the direction of the retina and the other goes off in the direction of the toenail. This is one of God's highest-quality tricks, and many world-class biologists would give up tenure just to know exactly how He pulls it off.

The secret of this differentiation—which will eventually result in over 200 different kinds of tissue and organ cells—is somehow mysteriously locked up in the DNA. Within each cell are chromosomes consisting of tightly coiled DNA, and encoded within this DNA are instructions on how to recreate the entire human body. This initial single-cell DNA, which determines everything from your handedness to eye color to foot size to whether you are at risk of premature heart disease, weighs 0.2 millionths of a millionth of an ounce. The *combined initial* single-cell DNA of every person alive today (all six billion) would weigh one thousandth of an ounce.[3]

With that introduction, let's spotlight more directly this amazing story and see what we can discover about the power and sovereignty of God.

The Chromosomes, Genes, and DNA

As we turn our microscope deep within each cell we find a nucleus. Inside the nucleus we discover twenty-three pairs of chromosomes staring back at us. These chromosomes are not the only structures in the nucleus, but they are the superstars, and I think they know it. They stand out like Michael Jordan in the midst of a fourth grade basketball team. They have been getting a lot of press lately, with good reason.

These twenty-three pairs of chromosomes—one-half contributed from the maternal egg and one-half contributed from the paternal sperm—contain 100 thousand genes. If you connect all these twenty-three pairs together (at least figuratively) you will have the total genetic structure of the human body. This single combined mega-chromosome is called the human genome. The Human Genome Project, begun in 1990, is an ambitious, multi-year, multi-billion-dollar, multi-nation undertaking to "map" the position of each gene on the human genome.[4]

Envision this human genome as a very, very, very, very, very long twisted strand consisting of two thin pieces of filament. These filaments are the two strands of DNA. They are wound tightly together in what is called a double helix. It was the discovery of this molecular model of twisted-ladder DNA in 1953 that later won Francis Crick and James Watson the Nobel Prize.

The double helix DNA is constructed of three fundamental repeating ingredients: a sugar, a phosphate, and a base. The sugar and the phosphate combine to form the backbone of the long DNA molecule, while the bases form its side chains. In other words, the sugar and phosphate make up the length of the ladder and the bases are the horizontal rungs.

The sugar and the phosphate are always the same, but there are four different bases, which we will call A, C, G, and T.[5] The chain of DNA is built by linking these base pairs, rather like God playing with Legos. For example, at one level you might have an A linked to a T; then at the next level you might find a C linked to a G; and you just keep linking and building, up and up, for a very long way. There are *three billion* such base pairings that make up the human genome, leading to a staggering level of mathematical and biochemical complexity. Lest you are still unimpressed, consider the following:

- If we were to take all of the DNA out of a single cell and stretch it out, it would be over five feet long.[6]
- This same DNA is so thin that it is only 50 trillionths of an inch wide.[7]
- A strand of DNA stretched to the sun would weigh only one-fiftieth of an ounce.[8]
- It you were to take this single-cell DNA and compress it down, it would be tinier than a speck of invisible dust.
- If you took all the DNA from all the cells in the body and squeezed it together, it would fit inside an ice cube.[9]
- If you were to take this same DNA from all the cells and stretch it out end to end, it would reach 10 billion miles (at minimum; the maximum estimated range is 170 billion miles).[10]

The purpose of the chromosomes and DNA is to carry the genes. And the purpose of the genes is to make proteins. And the purpose of the proteins is to . . . well, to do everything. "A typical cell," explains biochemist Michael Behe, author of the award-winning *Darwin's Black Box*, "contains thousands and thousands of different types of proteins to perform the many tasks necessary for life, much like a carpenter's workshop might contain many different kinds of tools for various carpentry tasks."[11] Each gene knows how to make one specific protein. Thus if there are 100 thousand genes, there are also about 100 thousand different proteins. "The best way to look at it is that a gene is like a sentence in an encyclopedia," explains geneticist Maxine Singer. "The gene instructs the cell how to do some one thing."[12]

These proteins are made from twenty different amino acids. Some proteins are simple and need only a short span of the human genome to instruct for their duplication. Other proteins are enormously complex and take a great length of genetic material for their duplication. The DNA performs well with either demand—short protein or long protein. It is like a computer, copy machine, and Encyclopaedia Britannica combined.

The capacity and performance of the DNA is impressive. If the DNA sequence of the human genome were compiled into thousand-page books (the size of a Manhattan telephone directory), the equivalent of 200 volumes would be needed to hold it all. To read a person's genome sequence out loud without stopping at a rate of ten bases per second (A, T, C, G, A, T, C, G, A, T, and so on) would take 9½ years to finish. At a more realistic pace of three bases per second (rather than ten per second) and a forty-hour reading week (rather than nonstop reading twenty-four hours a day), it would take 132 years to finish.[13]

Of DNA, Mutations, Evolution, and First Things

Only 10 percent of the DNA is used for coding the proteins. We are not completely sure what role the other 90 percent plays. Some of it might be control sequence, some of it might be debris, and undoubtedly at least a portion of it carries a run-down of intercellular baseball scores and most actively traded liver stocks.

In addition, a portion of this extra DNA guards against faulty copies. Obviously with a job this big—copying three billion base pairs at a time, trillions of times a day—there are bound to be mistakes. The DNA has its own spell-checker of sorts, an enzyme that examines the newly copied DNA for errors. When an error is found, that segment is replaced. If the error is not found and corrected, the resulting flawed DNA then carries a "mutation." This is thought to be the mechanism (at least in part) behind many birth defects, cancer, and aging.

Usually the DNA replication occurs with remarkable accuracy, making only one error in a billion copy steps.[14] Nevertheless, each of us carries about half a dozen defective genes. This does not mean that we have genetic disease, but only that we all have some degree of defect in our genetic sequencing. In fact, nearly 100 percent of us carry genetic defects of some type, but only about 10 percent of us has or will develop an inherited genetic disorder. The reason we are protected is redundancy. Because we carry two copies of every gene—one from the mother and one from the father—in the majority of cases one normal gene is sufficient to avoid all the symptoms of genetic disease.[15]

Evolutionists trust — as a matter of fact, they *totally rely on* — this process of mutation for the development and advancement of all species. The *theory of first things* goes like this: first you start with nothing, which then becomes something. The something then becomes a prebiotic soup with hydrogen, carbon, nitrogen, and water vapor (free oxygen arrives later). The soup bubbles into compounds like methane and ammonia. Lightning strikes periodically, stirring the pot. This frightens various molecules into each other's arms. Eventually, after this happens enough, you get an amino acid. Then several. These get frightened into each other's arms (they don't like lightning either), and you get a protein. Then larger and larger proteins. Then more and more of them. And pretty soon (well, actually, not so soon) you have an organism with a hundred thousand proteins made by a DNA that has three billion base pairs — all because of random beneficent mutations. When the pot stops bubbling and the smoke clears, out of the cave steps Arnold Schwarzenegger: tens of trillions of cells with a hundred billion neurons, sixty thousand miles of blood vessels, and a retina that in a fraction of a second solves nonlinear differential equations that would take a Cray-2 supercomputer a hundred years to solve.

It is all so intuitive, so straightforward, so reasonable. One wonders how people can be so naive as not to see what is so obvious.

In fact, evolutionary theory that depends on nothing but time + matter + energy + chance has problems at almost every step in the above sequence (an extremely hostile prebiotic soup and the juggernaut of irreducible complexity, to cite but a few). In the context of this discussion about DNA, complexity, information, order, and design, let's examine just two of the problems associated with strict evolutionary naturalist theory: time and mathematical probability.

Time — All life on earth, whether bacteria, bee, bear, or boy, is DNA-based. How non-life first stepped across the magical threshold and became life — something that uses nutrition, discards waste, reproduces itself, and stores DNA-based information — is yet unknown by evolutionary microbiologists. This is not a small step but a gaping gulf: instead of stepping from our back yard to the porch, it is stepping from the earth to the moon. In the words of Australian microbiologist Michael Denton: "Between a living cell and the most highly ordered non-biological system, such as a crystal or a snowflake, there is a chasm as vast and absolute as it is possible to conceive."[16]

Still, here we are today, alive on planet earth, so . . . *something* must have gotten us here, right? The fallback position for many evolutionary theorists is time. Given enough time, they argue, anything can happen. And when you postulate billions of years, well, that certainly sounds like enough time. If you just keep saying it over and over, and louder and louder, and you pile up a few Ph.D.s behind your name, then people finally say "I guess it seems reasonable to me"—even if they don't really have a clue about its actual reasonableness.

Let me at this point borrow from Gerald L. Schroeder, an orthodox Jewish biblical scholar, who earned a Ph.D. in physics from Massachusetts Institute of Technology before moving to Jerusalem to further his study of the Torah and teach at the Weizmann Institute. In his book *The Science of God*, Schroeder explains how the "time solves everything" argument was claimed in 1954 by Harvard biology professor and Nobel laureate George Wald in a *Scientific American* article entitled "The Origin of Life":

> However improbable we regard this event [the start of all life], or any of the steps which it involves, given enough time it will almost certainly happen at least once. And for life as we know it . . . once may be enough.
>
> Time is in fact the hero of the plot. The time with which we have to deal is of the order of two billion years. What we regard as impossible on the basis of human experience is meaningless here. Given so much time the "impossible" becomes the possible, the possible prob-able, and the probable virtually certain. One has only to wait: time itself performs the miracles.[17]

It sounded authoritative, and who is going to argue with a Harvard Nobelist? The only trouble is, it was wrong. So wrong, in fact, that twenty-five years later *Scientific American* made the rather shocking decision to print an unequivocal retraction:

> Although stimulating, this article probably represents one of the very few times in his professional life when Wald has been wrong. Examine his main thesis and see. Can we really form a biological cell by waiting for chance combinations of organic compounds? Harold Morowitz, in his book *Energy Flow and Biology,* computed that merely to create a bacterium would require more time than the Universe might ever see if chance combinations of its molecules were the only driving force.[18]

Since 1979, observes Schroeder, reputable scientific journals no longer accept articles that cite the origin of life as rising from random reactions over billions of years. "Confirmed evolutionists agree that you just cannot win if the classic concept of *randomness* at the point molecular level of DNA is the driving force behind the mutations. The time is just not there."[19]

Time, it seems, doesn't perform miracles. That is still God's department (including that clever trick when He reached into a hat and pulled out time itself).

Mathematical probability—Why did time fail the hopeful evolutionist? Time failed because it could not pass the probability test. The origin of life appears theologically suggestive via the probability (and related complexity) argument, just as the striking informational nature of DNA looks theologically suggestive via the probability (and related complexity) argument. Let's look at the evidence.

- Marcel P. Schutzenberger of the University of Paris, in calculating the probability of evolution based on mutation and natural selection, concluded that "there is no chance ($<10^{-1000}$) to see this mechanism appear spontaneously and if it did, even less for it to remain."[20]
- Molecular biophysicist Harold Morowitz calculated that if one were to take the simplest living cell and

break every chemical bond within it, the odds that the cell would reassemble under ideal natural conditions would be $10^{-100,000,000,000}$.[21]

- Astrophysicist Edward Argyle calculated the probability that even a simple organism arose on the early earth by chance. "It would seem impossible," he wrote, "for the prebiotic earth to have generated more than about two hundred bits of information, an amount that falls short of the six million bits in *E. coli* (a bacteria) by a factor of 30,000." (The *E. coli* having an information content of six million bits means that it would require $10^{1,800,000}$ different possible cases or states for its inception to occur.)[22]

- Writes John Horgan in *Scientific American*: "Some scientists have argued that, given enough time, even apparently miraculous events become possible—such as the spontaneous emergence of a single-cell organism from random couplings of chemicals. Sir Fred Hoyle, the British astronomer, has said such an occurrence is about as likely as the assemblage of a 747 by a tornado whirling through a junkyard. Most researchers agree with Hoyle on this point."[23]

- Physicists Fred Hoyle and Chandra Wickramasinghe calculated the odds that all the functional proteins necessary for life might form in one place by random events as one chance in $10^{40,000}$. They concluded that this was "an outrageously small probability that could not be faced even if the whole universe consisted of organic soup."[24]

- Thomas Huxley, in apparent support of the "time solves everything" thesis, once said that six monkeys typing randomly for millions of years would eventually type out all the books in the British Museum. Calculating the actual number of permutations of letters, lines, and pages in the 700,000 books in the British Museum in Huxley's time, cyberneticist David Foster concluded: "Huxley was hopelessly wrong in stating that six monkeys allowed enormous time would randomly type all the books in the British Museum when in fact they could only type half a line of one book if they typed for the duration of the universe."[25]

- Physicists Fred Hoyle and Chandra Wickramasinghe also did calculations that refuted Huxley: "Troops of monkeys thundering away at random on typewriters could not produce the works of Shakespeare, for the practical reason that the whole observable universe is not large enough to contain the necessary monkey hordes, the necessary typewriters, and certainly the waste paper baskets required for the deposition of wrong attempts. The same is true of living material."[26]

- A simple calculation, explains physicist Schroeder, can show that the likelihood of producing any particular sonnet of Shakespeare by random typing is about one chance in 10^{690}. "The statistical improbability of pure chance yielding even the simplest forms of life has made a mockery of the theory that random choice alone gave us the biosphere we see."[27]

- Continuing with the typing monkeys illustration, Schroeder further clarifies the problems with randomness. "First we notice that random generation of letters by a computer, or by the hypothetical monkeys typing away on typewriters, never produces meaningful sentences more than a few words in length. . . . There is essentially zero chance (actually in the order of one chance out of 10^{120}) that any one of the sentences from all the libraries of the world would be generated by random typing. Randomness just doesn't cut it when it comes to generating meaningful order out of chaos. Direction is required. Always."[28]

- In attempting to make a case for the possibility of extraterrestrial intelligence, Carl Sagan and Francis Crick estimated that the difficulty of evolving a human by chance processes alone is $10^{-2,000,000,000}$. (ET, phone earth. Please!)[29]

■ "While many outside origin-of-life biology may still invoke 'chance' as a causal explanation for the origin of biological information, few serious researchers still do," explains Stephen C. Meyer, who earned his Ph.D. in the history and philosophy of science from Cambridge University. "Since molecular biologists began to appreciate the sequence specificity of proteins and nucleic acids, many calculations have been made to determine the probability of formulating functional proteins and nucleic acids at random. . . . Such calculations have invariably shown that the probability of obtaining functionally sequenced biomacromolecules at random is, in [Nobelist Ilya] Prigogine's words, 'vanishingly small'. . . . Chance is not an adequate explanation for the origin of biological complexity and specificity."[30]

There are more illustrations of the probability problem—in fact, many more. But the point is that neither *time* nor *chance* can solve the naturalist's probability problem. Everywhere we see life—from simple to highly developed forms—we see order. This order involves coded information in the form of DNA. Any serious thinker is confronted with two unavoidable questions: *How did non-life first step across the threshold to become life? And how did life encode immensely complex amounts of information on DNA?* Time + chance has no answers for these questions. Randomness is a non-starter, not a solution.

"Our experience with information-intensive systems indicates that such systems always come from an intelligent source—i.e., from mental or personal agents, not chance," explains Dr. Meyer.

During the last forty years, every naturalistic model proposed has failed to explain the origin of information. . . . Thus, mind or intelligence or what philosophers call "agent causation," now stands as the only cause known to be capable of creating an information-rich system, including the coding regions of DNA, functional proteins, and the cell as a whole.[31]

This is not to assume that God needs us to mount a statistical defense of His sovereignty. But it is only to say that if we observe design, it is not wrong to infer a Designer. If we observe life, it is not wrong to infer a Life-giver. If we see DNA, it is not wrong to infer the precision of a Genius. If we see information and intelligence and intention, it is not wrong to infer that "behind the dim unknown, standeth God within the shadow, keeping watch above his own."[32]

DNA, Bioethics, and Designer Genes

Before leaving the topic of DNA as it relates to God's sovereignty it is important to pay a glancing visit to the future of bioethics, including such issues as the Human Genome Project, gene therapy, stem-cell and germ-cell manipulation, genetic engineering and eugenics, cloning, and the attempt to create life. The word *sovereign* applied to God is not only a label but also a title. His possessing such a title means we need to be careful about invading His DNA turf unless permission is granted beforehand.

The answers to these issues are not easy, and I do not wish to be theologically simplistic or ethically legalistic. But I would be less than honest if I didn't express my deep concerns about what this all will mean for collective humanity. God surely has an opinion about such things, even though the Scriptures are not always theologically clear about what that opinion might be.

Let's explore some generalizations before moving to specifics.

First, it is inevitable that as a society, a nation, and a world we will relentlessly pursue biogenetic research and intervention. This inevitability is fixed. The forward thrust of progress and knowledge acquisition is both powerful and unstoppable. The scientific knowledge and engineering technology will be here before we know it—and surely before we are ethically prepared for the consequences.

Second, these things will be presented to us as a benefit, a promise. Such developments arrive at our doorstep looking more like Dr. Schweitzer and Mother Theresa than Hitler and Frankenstein. Our future ability to treat a wide range of diseases through gene therapy, for example, will be almost beyond imagination. A current ad for a biotechnology company shows a picture of the DNA double-helix molecule with the immodest caption "At the top of this ladder is a world without disease." To eventually alleviate suffering through relatively simple genetic interventions seems not only humanitarianly sound but almost morally imperative.

Third, despite the fact that these issues will be presented in a positive light, the final result will be mixed. We will experience both positive and negative consequences together. Whatever humans use, we also abuse. Everyone involved in the biotechnology frontier recognizes such a potential. But not everyone agrees about the degree of danger that awaits us or the degree of caution thus warranted. Fearful pessimists insist we should forbid all activity in human genome biotechnology. Hopeful optimists think we should free-float and let the issues work themselves out over time.

The following brief synopses offer a glimpse of what the near future will hold.

Human Genome Project—Holding the completed human genome in our hand will represent one of the deepest penetrations yet of humankind into understanding the fundamental mysteries of life, with all the positive and negative implications inherent in such a statement. Once we have available the technology to print out all 100 thousand of our genes, what will we do with such potential knowledge? Would you want to know if you have the gene for a certain disease? Would you want to know if you have the gene for a *tendency* toward a certain disease (a much more complex question)? Who would pay for testing, or for screening? Would screening be conducted for all genetic disorders, or only selected ones? Will potential employers insist on such information prior to offering a contract? Will insurance companies insist on such information prior to offering a policy? Will parents wish to obtain a full genome of their developing baby—obtained, for example, by chorionic-villus sampling at ten weeks gestation? Will they choose abortion even for minor imperfections? Will attorneys sue physicians who don't offer such tests if a child is born with a genetic disease? None of these questions has socially stable answers.

Gene therapy—Gene therapy essentially means slipping a healthy gene into the cells of one organ of a patient suffering from a genetic disease. The first human case was in 1990, and the initial experience was disappointing. Recently, however, the record of success has been brighter. "Twenty years from now gene therapy will have revolutionized the practice of medicine," predicts Dr. W. French Anderson, director of gene therapy at the University of Southern California Medical School. "Virtually every disease will have gene therapy as one of its treatments."[33] This road, however, will lead all the way to "designer babies," where genetic structures will be placed within the genome of an embryo prior to being implanted into the mother's womb.

Another variant of the same general theme is a process called *pre-implantation genetic diagnosis (PGD)*, where the mother's egg and father's sperm are mixed in a Petri dish and the resultant fertilized eggs are subjected to intense DNA analysis. Only those that pass the genetic tests are implanted. Says Dr. Jeffrey Botkin of the University of Utah: "Instead of aborting a fetus, you're flushing down a bunch of 16-cell embryos—which, to a lot of folks [who oppose abortion], is a lot less of a problem."[34]

Stem-cell manipulation—Embryonic stem cells are those that exist prior to the primitive cell's differentiation into more than 200 types of specialized cells. By working with these pre-differentiated cells (usually taken from early abortions), scientists hope to grow organs for transplant on demand, among other applications. Human embryonic stem cells, first isolated at the University of Wisconsin and Johns Hopkins University in 1999, have been called "immortal" because with the help of an enzyme called telomerase, they appear to subdivide endlessly.[35]

Germ-cell manipulation—Genetic therapy in germline cells has the potential to affect not only the individual being treated, but his or her children as well. "Germline therapy would change the genetic pool of the entire human species, and future generations would have to live with that change," explains one biotechnology corporation.[36]

Genetic engineering and eugenics—Some futurists predict biotechnology will "alter the course of human evolution." Princeton biologist Lee Silver predicts the creation of super-races genetically enhanced for physical prowess or superior intelligence.[37]

Cloning—The cloning of humans *will* happen. This is not an *if* issue, but a *when* issue. Once the technology is fully available (and some suggest the technology is already here), then it is only a matter of time. As someone observed, the song "There'll Never Be Another You" might no longer be true.

> First, choose an egg cell—any egg cell will do.
> Next, remove all the chromosomes from the nucleus.
> Set the egg aside and save for later use.
> Discard the chromosomes.
> Next select an adult cell from a Nobel physicist—any adult cell will do.
> Remove the chromosomes from this cell.
> Carefully transfer these "Nobelist chromosomes" to the egg cell.
> Place egg cell in uterus.
> Bake at 99 degrees for nine months or until brilliant.

Creating life?—Geneticists from the Institute for Genomic Research are experimenting with the minimal number of genes necessary for life (the "minimal gene set"). They began by selecting a tiny microorganism with a mere 470 genes, and then started removing one gene at a time. By so doing, they discovered that 170 of the individual genes were not essential for the life of the microorganism. However, if all 170 were removed, the microorganism did not survive. So they began adding the genes back one at a time to see if they could arrive at a level when, by adding one gene, they go from non-life to life. Recognizing the ethical importance of this experiment, the geneticists invited twenty ethicists, theologians, and philosophers to pull their beards and cross their eyes before the research proceeded. Bioethicist Arthur Caplan of the University of Pennsylvania commented: "I think what they discover will be a threat to the view that there is some magic, secret, outside force creating this thing called life."[38]

Jurassic Park meets *Brave New World*, coming soon to a theater near you:

- Journalists are writing seriously about the "possibility of virgin births, resurrecting the dead, and women giving birth to themselves."[39]
- Cow eggs had the bovine genetic material replaced with that of a pig and grew seventy pig embryos, giving rise to the question "Could a cow give birth to a human baby?"[40]
- Advanced Cell Technology reported that it had made a semi-human embryo by putting DNA from one of its scientist's cells into a cow's egg with bovine DNA removed.[41]
- Human genes have been put within cloned sheep, making them a "drug factory."
- The French cult Raelian Movement has formed a Bahamas-based company called CLONAID, the world's first commercial human cloning service. For "as low as $200,000" CLONAID will provide a cloned child to anyone wishing it, including "parents with fertility problems or homosexual couples." If a man should die early in life, "imagine the joy of a widow raising a child looking like her beloved deceased husband." Did anyone say Oedipal complex? This cult believes that life on earth was created scientifically in laboratories by extraterrestrials whose name (Elohim) is found in the Hebrew Bible and was mistranslated as the word "God." It also claims that Jesus' resurrection was a cloning performed by the Elohim. For a $50,000 fee, they will provide INSURACLONE, the sampling and storage of cells from a loved one to be cloned later if the beloved person dies unexpectedly. Farfetched? They expect one million cloning customers.[42]

The above is but a partial accounting of the future ethical fog rolling down from the mountaintops. I don't know if you can get a sense of the historic nature of it all, but we are playing with an explosive never before touched by human hands, while still not quite sure of God's opinion on the matter. Before venturing into such a playground, I think it best to stop first at the gate and ask God: "Do you mind if I play?"

The SKIN, STOMACH, SKELETON, *and* SPERM

WHAT God accomplished in creating the human body would have won Him Nobel Prizes in biology, chemistry, and physics every year for eternity—plus undoubtedly a couple of Emmys for most entertaining sitcom. Even though we have visited perhaps the most exciting destinations on our human design tour, there are still a few more points of interest to be considered. It would seem unappreciative of His efforts if we did not pause to regard these additional displays of His impressive workmanship.

Integumentary System

Skin—Although we seldom think of it as such, the skin is the largest organ of the body. It weighs eight or nine pounds and has a surface area of over two square yards. The skin performs remarkable services. For one, it keeps all the water inside. Our bodies are 60 percent water, and were it not for the skin we would quickly puddle the floor.

Yet "keeping the water in" is a much more complex process than it appears. The skin must keep *almost* all of the water in, while allowing some to escape, through sweating, for temperature control. In addition, it must be waterproof from the outside as well. "If I had to choose skin's most crucial contribution," explains world renowned leprosy surgeon and author Paul Brand, "I might opt for waterproofing."[1]

Solvents and disinfectants that damage the cutaneous barrier can increase water loss up to seventy-five times. On an even more dramatic level, the breakdown of this important function of fluid balance is the reason severe burns can be so deadly. Many people who die acutely from extensive burns succumb to dehydration. With the protective skin destroyed, serous fluids escape out of the tissues, and with them escapes life itself.

The skin also protects against the invasion of harmful agents, including chemicals and microbes. Untold billions of bacteria reside on our skin, most of them benignly, yet a few maliciously. The skin is an unyielding and vigilant guard.

Our skin color, controlled by melanocytes and melanin, is determined primarily by a mere four to six genes—that is, four to six genes out of the total 100 thousand. It seems a bit unfair that less than one-hundredth of one percent of our genetic structure is coded for differences in skin color, yet the results often seem like more than 99.99 percent.

Skin sensitivity to touch varies greatly. Pinching the ear is relatively painless but pricking the fingertip is annoying. Some segments of skin have thousands of nerve receptors per square inch. The pain communicated through these receptors is in fact an important benefit saving us from repeated traumatic and thermal damage.

Skin cells are continuously turning over—billions every day. The epidermis is replaced every couple of weeks, which is thus the duration of a suntan or super glue spill. Over a lifetime we each shed forty pounds of dead skin, perhaps explaining why old sofas weigh so much.

Youthful skin is remarkably elastic. As the skin ages, however, it loses elasticity due to changes in collagen. With the loss of elasticity, facial expressions begin to etch permanent lines. It has been estimated that it takes 200 thousand frowns to make a permanent line.[2] The structural fingerprint grooves are highly individual-specific, causing Scotland Yard to introduce them as a criminal detection classification in 1901.

Blood flow to the skin can vary tremendously—in some areas by a factor of 150 times. This is important for the crucial temperature control of the body but also plays a role in social blushing. Blushing is a function of dramatically increased blood flow to the skin surface, most notably of the face. It is involuntary and for those so prone, it cannot be controlled. Humans are the only creatures that have this capacity. Jeremiah talked, however, about a sinfulness so deep that "they have no shame at all; they do not even know how to blush."[3]

Blushing, however, was not responsible for Moses' changed appearance when he descended from Mount Sinai, for after meeting with God "the skin of his face shone."[4] The people were appropriately impressed. Until they forgot.

Sweat glands—As mentioned, the skin plays a vital role in temperature regulation both through conductive heat loss (by shunting blood to the body's surface) and through perspiration. About a pint of water is undetectably lost through the skin every day, called *insensible perspiration*. When the thermometer is blistering, however, the amount of water lost increases dramatically. It is possible to lose as much as two gallons a day through overt perspiration. If this sweating mechanism breaks down during vigorous exercise on a hot day, core body temperatures can shoot up rapidly and death by heat stroke becomes a serious threat.

Humans have several different types of skin glands, but the most infamous (that is, odoriferous) are the eccrine sweat glands. A single square inch of the palm can contain three thousand such glands, while the soles of the feet have a total of one-quarter million.

We may wonder why such a classy God would choose such a sweaty mechanism for temperature control. Surely His design options were not limited to only this one possibility. Yet despite whatever physical discomfort and social embarrassment accompanies perspiration, it is an effective mechanism. Maybe God is trying to teach us that social acceptability based on superficial issues isn't quite as important to Him as it is to us. And of course, we also must contend with that penalizing verse in Genesis: "By the sweat of your brow you will eat your food until you return to the ground."[5]

Hair—Human hair, as strong as aluminum, grows on all portions of the body except the palms and soles. There are five million hair follicles in the body, including one hundred thousand hair follicles on the scalp alone. Combining the activity of all these scalp follicles together, they grow one thousand inches of hair each day. Individually over its lifetime, each follicle will produce twenty-six feet of hair. Collectively over this same duration, the scalp will produce nearly five hundred miles of hair.

The hair follicles of each anatomic region have their own unique growth and rest cycles. On the head, for example, hair follicles have a growing cycle of between two and seven years, followed by a rest cycle of three months. During the growth cycle, the hair will experience daily lengthening. During the rest cycle, the hair will maintain the same length for the duration. When the next growth cycle begins, a new hair erupting from the follicle punches out the old hair. Thus we naturally lose 50 to 125 hairs per day.

We tend to place a fair amount of emphasis on our hair. While at a certain level this is not wrong, we should always be asking prioritizing questions about such behavior. The apostle Peter advised: "Your beauty should not come from outward adornment, such as braided hair and the wearing of gold jewelry and fine clothes. Instead, it should be that of your inner self, the unfading beauty of a gentle and quiet spirit, which is of great worth in God's sight."[6] To me, there is no greater beauty than the beauty that comes from purity.

In *The Penitent,* author and Nobel laureate Isaac Bashevis Singer tells the story of a man who experiences prosperity yet also profound emptiness in the U.S. During a search for meaning, he flees to Israel only to find an extension of the same materialist emptiness. Finally he discovers fulfillment in Jewish orthodoxy.

On one occasion, he sits at dinner in the home of a rabbi. Inquiring about the rabbi's children, he discovers all have died except one. The sole remaining child is a young widow who lives nearby. At just that moment she unexpectedly comes for a visit.

> Just as we sat talking, the door opened and in came a young woman with a kerchief over her head. She looked no more than eighteen, but I later learned she was twenty-four. One look sufficed to tell me a lot about her: first of all, that hers was a rare beauty, not the kind fashioned in beauty parlors, but the beauty and charm that's given by God.
>
> Secondly, I saw that she glowed with the grace of chastity. The concept that the eyes are the windows of the soul is not a mere figure of speech. You can see in a person's eyes whether he is full of arrogance or modesty, honesty or cunning, pride or humility, fear of God or abandon. This young woman's eyes reflected all . . . the great qualities mentioned in *The Path of Righteousness.*[7]

There is beauty . . . and then there is beauty. One is provided by "outward adornment, such as braided hair and the wearing of gold jewelry and fine clothes" and is highly valued by social norms. The other is provided by the "inner self, the unfading beauty of a gentle and quiet spirit" and is highly valued by God Himself.

Nails and teeth—Nails and teeth come from the same embryonic layers as do skin and hair. Perhaps the ancients understood embryology better than we give them credit for, as when Job said: "I have escaped with only the skin of my teeth."[8]

Nails grow slowly. At about two inches a year, this rate is only slightly less than the rate at which Mount Everest is moving toward China (two and a half inches a year).[9] Cumulatively during our lifetime we grow almost 100 feet of fingernails.

The teeth are made up of four types of material, including enamel, the strongest substance in the body. It is ironic that such seemingly impenetrable materials should be so susceptible to decay. Perhaps this is the dental equivalent of "Let any one who thinks that he stands take heed lest he fall."[10] Bacteria react with carbohydrates in the mouth to form acids capable of dissolving the enamel. The breakdown of the enamel permits other bacteria to penetrate the dentin, eventually producing a cavity. Once this process begins, teeth do not have the capacity to repair themselves.

The teeth appear so strong, shiny, and straight. That's one moment. But in the next, they can break in an unexpected injury. Or, insidiously, they can crumble from slow, steady internal decay. In the same way, God can break us: "You have broken the teeth of the wicked," wrote David.[11] Or He can leave us alone and allow the decaying process of sin to bring internal corrosion. Either way the knee will be bowed. In referring to Himself as the cornerstone, Jesus offered this interesting verse: "Everyone who falls on that stone will be broken to pieces, but he on whom it falls will be crushed."[12] One way or the other, we all will be broken.

Jesus often referred to that time of judgment where there would be "weeping and gnashing of teeth."[13] I don't know exactly what gnashing of teeth is, but from the sound of it, I think I'd rather be elsewhere.

Digestive System

All human activities, even rest, require energy (see Figure 2). To provide this needed energy, our bodies require the periodic intake of nutrition, just as an automobile's engine requires an occasional fill-up at the pump. The digestive system takes this raw "fuel" in the form of food, processes it, and sends it to the cells, where biochemical processes convert it into usable fuel for the tiny cellular biofires.

Figure 2—Under resting conditions the body's energy consumption is used principally by:[14]	
Liver and spleen	27%
Skeletal muscles and heart	25%
Brain	19%
Kidneys	10%
Other, including the digestive system	19%

The digestive system is perhaps more "linear" than other complex body processes, acting at times like a simple hollow tube.

But don't underestimate it, for it is in fact extraordinarily complex. It involves many organs and numerous wide-ranging chemicals and enzymes. The beginning-to-end process is already generally well known, so we will only highlight the more striking aspects of this system.

The average stomach has about a one-quart capacity. Throughout the day, however, it produces over three quarts of gastric fluid, including hydrochloric acid in a concentration strong enough to cause tissue damage. That the muscular stomach does not digest itself is remarkable.

As the food passes through the pylorus of the stomach, it enters the twenty-two-foot-long small intestine. Here digestive enzymes are added and most of the work of absorption is performed. Because of the extreme redundancy of innumerable tiny, finger-like projections called *villi* and even smaller *microvilli*, the overall absorptive surface area of the small intestine equals that of a tennis court.

The small intestines contain not only chemical enzymes and large surface areas, but also what has been called a *second brain*. "Structurally and neurochemically, the enteric nervous system (ENS) is a brain unto itself," explains cell biologist Michael D. Gershon.[15] The nutrition-to-energy process is so essential to our survival that God apparently did not trust it to the simple principles of mechanics.

Soon after entering the small intestine, food passes the sphincter where the liver and gall bladder add their contributions. Next to the skin, the football-sized three-pound liver is the largest organ of the body. Its 300 billion cells perform over 500 functions. The gall bladder, tucked under the liver almost as if it were hiding from the chest cavity, releases more than a pint of bile every day (the bile itself is actually made in the liver but stored in the gall bladder). While the gall bladder is surgically expendable, the presence of a healthy liver is not optional.

All of the blood flowing away from the stomach and intestines must first pass through the liver before reaching the rest of the body. The liver is thus situated at a crucial crossroads, entailing countless responsibilities. It detoxifies substances, guards vitamin and mineral supplies, stockpiles sugar, produces quick energy, manu-factures new proteins, regulates clotting factors, controls cholesterol, makes bile, maintains hormone balance, stores iron, assists immune function, and is even responsible for making the fetal blood cells in the womb. One thing it does *not* do is complain. It will work and work without protest, even under enormous abuse.[16]

More than any other organ in the body, the liver has tremen-dous regenerative properties. Actually, liver cells rarely reproduce themselves in a healthy body—all of their attention is given to the myriad of tasks that cannot be performed by any other tissue. However, when a part of the liver is injured or destroyed, the remaining healthy cells go into Amish barn-building mode. In such a crisis, "virtually all of the surviving hepatocytes leave their normal, growth-arrested state and proliferate until the destroyed part of the liver is replaced," explain hepatologists Anna Mae Diehl, M.D., and Clifford Steer, M.D., of the American Liver Foundation. "Amazingly, the liver is generally able to perform its usual functions, even when large fractions of hepatocytes are actively replicating."[17]

The liver's remarkable ability to regenerate was noted even in ancient times. "Remember," observe Diehl and Steer, "Zeus punished his enemy by chaining Prometheus to a rock and ordering a bird of prey to devour his liver daily. Aware that the liver could regenerate overnight, Zeus had devised a plan that would damn Prometheus to eternal torture without allowing him to escape by death."[18]

The six-inch pancreas also joins the plumbing at the same point as the liver and gall bladder. In addition to producing impor-tant digestive enzymes, it also contains small groups of cells called the islands of Langerhans. These specialized cells produce the insulin that regulates blood sugar levels.

The large intestine has as its main activity the absorption of water, sodium, and other minerals. Once any remaining food par-ticles enter the colon, the brakes are applied. Now in slow motion, every particle passing by is carefully inspected by the colonic lining. Here the mucosal cells have one last chance to salvage any useful ingredients that the body might need.

The digestive tract is a 95 percent efficient energy extractor. If we eat something rich in calories, it is unreasonable to hope that much of the caloric burden will not be absorbed. In fact, very little of the energy that we ingest fails to make its ultimate presence known within our weighted-down cells. It is wishful thinking to hope that irresponsible eating on our part will be overlooked by an inefficient design on God's part. He doesn't work that way.

We occasionally hear the accusation "their god is their stomach." It scarcely needs pointing out, however, that the god of gastroenterology cannot compete with the God of eternity. "God designed the human machine to run on Himself," explains C. S. Lewis. "He Himself is the fuel our spirits were designed to burn, or the food our spirits were designed to feed on. There is no other. That is why it is just no good asking God to make us happy in our own way without bothering about religion. God cannot give us a happiness and peace apart from Himself, because it is not there. There is no such thing."[19]

When the disciples encouraged Jesus to eat, He replied: "I have food to eat that you know nothing about. . . . My food . . . is to do the will of him who sent me."[20]

Musculoskeletal System
The adult human has 206 bones, a number 40 percent decreased since infancy due to the fusion of adjacent bones. Bones are a composition of mineral crystals (mostly calcium and phosphorus), collagen, and cells. The resultant material is as strong as granite in compression and twenty-five times stronger than granite under tension.[21]

People are routinely shocked to discover the pressure bones must withstand. Considering the twenty-six bones in each foot, orthopedist Dr. Brand observes that "a soccer player subjects these small bones to a cumulative force of over one thousand tons per foot over the course of a match."[22] The femur is stronger than reinforced concrete and must bear an average of 1,200 pounds of pressure per square inch with every step. The midshaft of the femur is capable of supporting a force of six tons before it fractures.[23]

Why are humans six feet tall and not sixty? For one reason, if we were sixty feet tall we would fracture our femur with every step—which would make going to get the mail feel like a rugby match. It is all a matter of geometry and gravity.[24] God no doubt had the math worked out with the original blueprint, and I'm glad He didn't misplace a decimal point.

Of interest (although of surprisingly little relevance to our skeletal system), the weight of the atmosphere pressing down on our shoulders is one ton. If it feels at times that we are supporting a huge load in life, we are. Yet it is not our bones that bear this burden, but instead the support of equal air pressure on all sides. Despite this scientific brush-off of atmospheric tonnage, in another sense we do indeed labor under another enormous weight— namely our own collective fallenness. What will it feel like, on the other side of eternity, to have this exhausting and painful daily weight removed?

Bone is living tissue with a vibrant blood and nerve supply. Yet by volume, only 2 percent of bone is made up of cells. These cells are capable of destroying old bone structure (the osteoclasts) and rebuilding new bone (the osteoblasts). Our skeleton, on average, replaces itself totally about every seven years.

After damage to the bone, osteoclasts are recruited to the site of injury where they resorb the impaired bone material. When their job is finished, the osteoclasts undergo programmed cell death. Next, osteoblasts are recruited to the site. They make layers of osteoid that slowly refills the cavity. When the osteoid reaches six microns thick (two ten-thousandths of an inch), it begins to mineralize. Even after the cavity has been filled with bone, still for months the crystals of mineral are packed more closely and the new bone density continues to increase.[25] When the process is complete, the bone will be as strong as before the original injury.

Of the two to four pounds of calcium in the body, nearly 99 percent is in the bones and teeth. The remaining 1 percent, however, is of critical importance in blood clotting, nerve transmission, muscle contraction, and heart function. The body keeps the blood level of calcium within a narrow range, and if needed, the bone releases it readily.[26] This is made possible by the exceptionally large total surface area of the tiny mineral crystals within the bone, equal to *one hundred acres!* Each of the small crystalline surfaces is exposed to a watery solution that permits the ready exchange of chemicals on demand.[27]

The core of many bones contains marrow, a remarkable blood cell factory that turns out a trillion cells daily. It produces red blood cells (with a life span of 120 days), platelets (with a life span of 6 days), and white blood cells (with a life span of 1 day or less). If blood loss occurs in the body, the marrow can dramatically increase the RBCs and platelets according to need. If infection threatens, the WBC numbers surge. Cells of the immune system also are initially derived from the bone marrow. In addition, the marrow contains a small number of invaluable stem cells that assure the continuation of future generations of marrow cells.

Where one bone is joined with another, the connecting tissue is called a ligament. Where a bone is joined to a muscle, the connecting tissue is called a tendon. The body's 200 bones and 600 muscles work together as integrated units, often hinged by joints. Just lifting a forkful of food from the plate to the mouth involves the use of more than thirty joints. If our spiritual sensitivity were sufficiently alert, the eye-brain-nerve-bone-joint-muscle coordination permitting such a movement would consistently inspire awe each time it was successfully completed.

The mechanism regulating muscle function is extraordinarily complex and still, after all these years, not completely understood. Perhaps we can agree together to skip the details (of myofibrils, filaments, sarcolemma, sarcoplasm, sarcoplasmic reticulum, A bands, I bands, H zone, Z line, actin, myosin, tropomyosin, troponin, myoglobin, ADP, ATP, creatine phosphate, pyruvic acid, lactic acid, membrane potential, myoneural junction, and motor end plates) and instead simply point out that the facial muscles are capable of seven thousand movements, that striated muscle can contract in one-tenth of a second, that jaw muscles can exert 200 pounds of pressure, and that the total tension that could be developed by all the muscles in the body of an adult man is nearly twenty-five tons.

Compare this to the best bionic efforts of engineers. In 1999, for example, NASA built the first artificial muscles and staged the world's first myo-bionic handshake. But the resultant "grip," generated by four polymer strips designed to bend in response to electrical charges, was barely noticeable.[28] God, with a twinkle in His eye, watched in amusement.

Additional Evidence of God's Genius

Everywhere we look in the human design we find displays of God's precision. No tissue, no organ system is so simplistic that it fails to elicit awe. And still we have not exhausted all the evidence available for us to uncover.

Each *kidney* has over one million nephrons, with each nephron being a complete urine-forming unit. The renal system receives 1,800 quarts of blood a day. In the glomeruli and tubules, the blood undergoes a sophisticated process of filtration and reabsorption. The glomeruli produce 190 quarts of filtrate daily, which is then passed on down the line to the tubules. In the tubules, 99 percent of the water (along with important chemicals and electrolytes) is reabsorbed. The final result is 1½ quarts of urine, thus removing from the body toxins and harmful byproducts of metabolism.

The kidneys play an important role in fluid conservation. Approximately 60 percent of our body is made up of *water*. The brain, for example, is 70 percent water, the skeletal muscle 75 percent, and the lung tissue nearly 90 percent. If we lose even as much as 3 percent of our total body water, the resultant dehydration causes both fatigue and dysfunction. The loss of 10 percent threatens life.

How did God do so much with plain water? It is not that He uses exotic ingredients to construct the body—in fact, He uses common materials. His secret lay in the brilliant use of design. To the non-integrationist, our body is three-fourths water and fat. To the theistic integrationist, however, we are much more. When we factor in the spark of the divine, the picture comes into focus. Instead of semi-organized piles of random fat and water, we are "fearfully and wonderfully made."[29] Even in his suffering Job understood: "Your hands shaped me and made me. . . . You gave me life and showed me kindness, and in your providence watched over my spirit."[30]

The *ovaries* contain two million primordial *eggs*, all formed before birth. Only about 400 of these will develop into maturity, one per month. The all-time record for childbirth was set by a Russian woman who produced sixty-nine children between the years 1725 and 1765.[31] There is reason to suspect it is one record that might yet stand for another 250 years.

The *sperm*, in contrast to the pre-formed egg cells, are produced each day — 120 million of them. Formed in the *testicles,* they are then stored in the redundant twenty-foot-long *epididymis.* An ejaculate can contain 200 to 400 million sperm. Of these, a few hundred thousand will reach the uterus; a thousand or so will reach the Fallopian tube; and about a hundred survive to reach the targeted egg cell.[32]

Once the winning sperm hits the egg cell, rapid chemical changes occur in the egg that preclude any other sperm from entering. At that point the DNA in the egg and sperm merge, finally settling on one unique individual configuration among tens of millions of genetic possibilities. Thus begins the miraculous construction of yet one more Image bearer.

We know from Christ's example that God is partial to little children. Is He perhaps then present in these early DNA details, at the exact moment of conception? I rather think so. "You knit me together in my mother's womb," said David.[33] Perhaps it is all simply too exciting for Him to stay away.

Our Body, *His* Temple

EVERY human body is a miracle exceeding comprehension. The complexity and dimensions involved are staggering to the mind, straining our abilities to apprehend the grandeur. Yet if we make the effort to reach for the meaning behind the biology, we will find ourselves edified on several levels.

First, we will see anew the *power* and *precision* of God. When we think of the majesty of God, we don't have to look through a telescope to the distant recesses of the universe—we need only look in the nearest mirror. If we doubt His abilities to help us with the intricacies of our day-to-day problems, we ought doubt no more. No human dilemma, no matter how convoluted or refractory, can begin to challenge God's demonstrated mastery of detail as seen in the previous chapters.

Second, we will be increasingly aware of the *intimacy* with which He carries out His creative efforts. This is a hands-on God, both in the creating and sustaining phases. He has not drifted off to sleep, nor is He preoccupied with some difficult problem on the other side of the universe. In fact, He watches over us more intimately than the human mind has the ability to perceive. Think of the red blood cell shed from the cross that had your name on it. Take a deep breath, and remember that you just inhaled 150 million air molecules that Jesus Himself breathed. Christ has a closeness and a familiarity with those for whom He died as He breathes new life into anyone willing to receive it.

Third, we will benefit from the reminder that God has a triple claim on us: as *creator, redeemer,* and *sustainer.* In light of such a claim we relinquish our bodies back, yielding to the One who cares more for us than we do for ourselves. In this yielding we find not defeat, but an unexpected freedom. May our surrender be a glad surrender.

God's Human Body Project
It is perhaps beneficial to collect the most impressive of God's human body accomplishments in one place and regard them all together. As we review, I might suggest that we develop a cumulative impression of what this picture reveals about the genius, power, sophistication, and artistry of God.

The human body is composed of ten thousand trillion trillion atoms—a number greater than the stars in the universe. In each person, more than a trillion of these atoms are replaced every one-millionth of a second.

These atoms, in turn, are comprised of subatomic particles, some of which have a life span of less than a billion billionth of a second. It is entirely possible that we have no subatomic bottom. As the technology becomes increasingly sophisticated, we discover yet smaller particles. We are, perhaps, infinite in the subatomic direction.

Each human cell is made up of a trillion atoms. The body contains between 10 and 100 trillion cells. We tear down and rebuild over a trillion cells every day. Each cell is remarkable in its own miniaturized way, with electric fields, protein factories, and hundreds of ATP energy motors 200 thousand times smaller than a pinhead.

In a lifetime, the heart beats over two billion times and pumps sixty million gallons of blood through sixty thousand miles of blood vessels. The smallest capillary vessels have seventy thousand square feet of surface area, a delicate wall several thousand times more fragile than toilet tissue. We each manufacture over two million red blood cells every second. Laid side by side, our red blood cells would stretch 100 thousand miles.

We breathe 600 million times over an average life span, with every breath containing over a billion trillion air molecules. These air molecules enter 300 million alveoli that provide a total surface area half the size of a tennis court. The hemoglobin in each red blood cell can carry a million molecules of oxygen to the cells.

The retina of the eye contains over 100 million rods and cones that take continuous pictures under light conditions that can vary by a factor of ten billion. Individual retinal photoelectric cells are so sensitive that they can be triggered by one billion-billionth the amount of light emitted by a flashlight. In one-third of a second, the retina solves the equivalent of nonlinear differential equations that would take a supercomputer 100 years to solve.

The ear has a million moving parts, can vibrate twenty thousand times per second, can hear sounds over a range of intensity that varies by a trillion, and can distinguish among two thousand different pitches. Sound waves that move the eardrum less than the diameter of a hydrogen molecule can be perceived by the brain, with the faintest sound audible having the negligible pressure of one ten-thousandth the push of a healthy mosquito. The ear can gauge the direction of a sound's origin based on a 0.00003 second difference in its arrival from one ear to the other, and it has a sophisticated balance mechanism containing 100 thousand hair cells.

The human nose can distinguish ten thousand different smells, including some chemicals present in only 1 part to 400 million parts air. We have nine thousand taste buds in our mouths and over 400 touch cells per square inch of skin. We can "feel" a pressure on our face that depresses the skin 0.00004 inch.

Our three-pound brain is the most complex arrangement of matter ever discovered in the universe. It contains ten billion neurons (possibly ten times as many) and has 100 trillion neurological interconnections that if stretched out would extend 100 thousand miles. The brain fires at a rate of a thousand trillion computations per second and can hold information equivalent to that contained in twenty-five million books. From Einstein to savants, we are known for prodigious feats of memory. Each of us carries around a mental videotape cassette containing three trillion pictures. We are the only species with the gift of language, are capable of thinking at a rate of 800 words per minute, and have *use* and *recognition* vocabularies of ten thousand and forty thousand words, respectively.

Billions of skin cells are replaced every day and the entire epidermis is replaced every couple of weeks. We each have five million hair follicles on our bodies and, in a lifetime, grow over two million feet of hair on our scalp.

Our twenty-two feet of small intestine has an absorptive surface area equal to that of a tennis court and is equipped with a "second brain." As an energy extractor, the digestive tract is 95 percent efficient. The liver has 300 billion cells that perform over 500 functions and can almost completely regrow itself if needed.

The adult human has over 200 bones that are as strong as granite in compression and twenty-five times stronger under tension. The femur is stronger than reinforced concrete, must bear an average of 1,200 pounds of pressure per square inch with every step, and is capable of supporting a force of six tons before it fractures. A soccer player bears a cumulative force exceeding one thousand tons per foot over the course of a match.

Our skeleton replaces itself totally about every seven years, contains a marrow that produces a trillion blood cells daily, and has a mineral crystal surface area of 100 acres, thus allowing for the quick exchange of calcium and other minerals as needed. We have over 600 muscles, including facial muscles capable of seven thousand movements. The total tension that can be developed by all the muscles of an adult man is nearly twenty-five tons.

Each kidney has over one million nephrons, and the renal system processes 1,800 quarts of blood a day. The female ovaries contain two million primordial eggs, all formed before birth. Only about 400 of these will develop into maturity. In contrast, the male produces over 100 million sperm each day, which are stored in the redundant twenty-foot-long epididymis. When the egg and sperm meet, the DNA must settle on one unique individual configuration among tens of millions of genetic possibilities.

The nucleus of this initial fertilized egg contains DNA-based chromosomes with 100 thousand genes and three billion base pairs. This initial single-cell DNA is over five feet long but only fifty-trillionths of an inch wide, weighing 0.2 millionth of a millionth of an ounce. The DNA from all the cells in one human body would stretch over ten billion miles.

From Dust to Honor

The biology involved is obviously stunning. What about the theology? Scripture teaches that we are made in God's very image, in His likeness.[1] We are made a little lower than the angels and crowned with glory and honor.[2]

God knows us even before He first forms our frame. He realizes that we are "dust," and knows that we are frail. He knows every word before it is on our tongue. He knows the thoughts of our mind and the intents of our heart. As it turns out, we were not just some science project for a rainy day in Heaven, but instead a creative effort treasured by the Father. He made us for His glory and His pleasure.

When we gain a picture of what this creative God has done within us, it helps us to understand that we are more than a random collection of organized atoms. Within the miracle of the human body, there is sanctity, hope, and glory. More important, this same awareness also helps us to appreciate that such a Creator is rightly regarded with awe.

When we see Him more clearly, we have more faith in His power and less anxiety about our circumstances. Our own frailty and finiteness seem less bothersome when we realize that we were designed by a God who can count to infinity backwards and recite the Encyclopaedia Britannica in every known human language in a trillionth of a second. If we have trouble understanding such things, perhaps we should reflect more on the meaning of the words *infinite* and *sovereign*.

A Temple, Incarnation, and Bride

This is the beginning of the story—but it is not the end. It turns out that God is not yet done with "the body." Before we leave human physiology to tour the cosmos, God has yet a few more things to teach us about His intentions for the body: as a temple, as an incarnation, and as a bride.

A temple—Our body, says the apostle Paul, is a temple of the Holy Spirit. Perhaps that is why God took such pains in design.

The definition of a temple is "a place where God dwells." In calling our body a temple, God is signaling that He desires to take up residence there. And why not? He created it; He sustains it; and He paid a great price to buy it back. Why can't He also inhabit it if He wishes? "Do you not know," wrote the apostle Paul, "that your body is a temple of the Holy Spirit, who is in you, whom you have received from God? You are not your own; you were bought at a price. Therefore honor God with your body."[3]

This presence of the Holy Spirit is not like that of an unwelcome houseguest, to be regarded with suspicion. He is not peering over our shoulders like a nagging relative ready to criticize the slightest flaw. Instead, this presence is a gift. Quite priceless, actually. If we had to pay the Holy Spirit a retainer for hanging around the temple, the wealthiest person on earth would not be able to afford the first minute's fee.

What is appropriate demeanor in a temple? If God is going to move in with us, how should we behave? Reverence and purity make a good start. A temple is to be kept holy and sacred. Because we personally have become a temple, we must now also become its spiritual custodian. We are therefore instructed to "honor God" with our bodies. Our bodies are to become a sacrifice. Not the dead-on-the-altar kind, but a living sacrifice, holy and pleasing to God.[4]

An incarnation—One of the most amazing mysteries of the universe is the incarnation—Christ becoming a human baby. How did the infinite God inhabit a finite physical body? It is perhaps an unsolvable question for mere mortals. Conceptually, it would be easier to fit the Pacific Ocean into a thimble than for the Infinite to become Mary's baby. It would be easier to reverse a full-blown atomic explosion than for the Immortal to put on mortality.

When Mary first discovered a child growing in her innocent

womb, undoubtedly her first thought was less than blissful. Understanding her natural anxiety, the angel comes to her in Luke 1, announcing God's intention and comforting her: "Do not be afraid. . . . He shall be great."[5] Indeed! But in Philippians 2, we read, "Your attitude should be the same as that of Christ Jesus: Who, being in very nature God . . . made himself nothing."[6]

So—both describing the same event—the angel says He shall be great, and Paul says that He made Himself nothing. Which was He . . . great or nothing? In usual parlance, there is a difference. When we meet someone great, we hire a band, have a parade, and throw a reception in a great hall. But we don't do that for a "nothing." Yet truly Jesus made Himself nothing. It was the only way infinity could become finite—through the nothingness gate. So, He emptied Himself. He was born with nothing, lived with nothing, and died with less than nothing. And God, who has the privilege of defining reality, proclaims that in this instance "nothing" and "great" are one and the same.

It seems to me that if we want to be great with God, the way to greatness is Christ's way: emptying ourselves, yielding ourselves up to Him, humbling ourselves and taking the nature of a servant, dying to self that He might live in us, making ourselves nothing so that He can give us worth. In this self-abandonment, God gives us greatness.

Yes, the Almighty became a baby. God, who created the body with such miraculous and even mystical flair, stooped to put on flesh and live within its frame. And when at last that body was broken, His brokenness accomplished our wholeness. His nothing was revealed as . . . everything.

A bride—God also regards the church universal as a body. It is called the *body of Christ,* and also the *bride of Christ.* This can seem unusual language, but God surely has His reasons.

Paul, again and again, reminds us that even though the church is made up of many people with various gifts, nevertheless we are to regard ourselves as one body. "Just as each of us has one body with many members, and these members do not all have the same function, so in Christ we who are many form one body, and each member belongs to all the others."[7]

One reason God chose to call the church a body is because it is such a perfect metaphor. But it goes beyond that. Is it possible that somehow, in a spiritually organic way, we indeed are all connected, networked together by a Spirit who has no trouble with such complexity? Is it possible that when one prays, everyone in the body benefits? That when one loves, everyone in the body is mysteriously lifted? That when one sins, everyone in the body takes the hit and feels the wound? I rather suspect so.

Mysterious, Miraculous

God always creates with several levels of meaning. He uses words precisely, with profound intentionality. Why did He put each of us in a body, and then put that body within a Body? There is something here for us, and it has to do with connectedness, dependence, order, and the common goal of life within Life.

The body. Never presume to fully understand it—physically, spiritually, or ecclesiastically. Instead, stand in awe at the kind of God who can package atoms in such a mystical, glorious form.

CHAPTER EIGHT

ENERGY, FORCE, MATTER, *and* GOD

PHYSICS, I have noticed, tends to intimidate people. Chemistry less so—but still daunting. Yet it is good to conquer this fear, for it is a fascinating time to be involved in these disciplines. Much is happening on these scientific fronts, all of it "theologically suggestive." It is hard to remain spiritually disinterested when God Himself is now teaching the class. One noted physicist commented: "If we need an atheist for a debate, I go to the philosophy department. The physics department isn't much use."[1] Einstein maintained that a "cosmic religious feeling" was the strongest motivation for scientific research.

Physics is the science of energy, force, matter, and their interactions. Chemistry is the science of the composition, structure, and properties of substances. Both point to God, causing British astronomer Fred Hoyle to complain that the universe looked like a "put up" job. Hoyle, no friend to theistic faith, continued by saying that "a common sense interpretation of the facts suggests that a superintellect has monkeyed with the physics, as well as chemistry."[2]

Let's investigate together and see what we can discover. If we can bring these daunting disciplines into the realm of comprehensibility, perhaps we can catch a glimpse of just what these new findings teach us about the genius and power of the Almighty Creator.

Beyond Our Abilities

Toward the beginning of the twentieth century, scientists thought there wasn't much left to learn about physics. The Newtonian world looked relatively simple, and the equations had all been discovered. Physicists perhaps thought of looking for other lines of work. That, however, was before relativity, quantum mechanics, the uncertainly principle, and superstrings.

Today, instead of feeling we know it all, we are afraid that we know nothing for sure. Instead of being certain of our facts, we suspect that almost nothing is as it seems. When a musical King of Siam sang: "There are times I almost think I am not sure of what I absolutely know," he could just as easily have been talking about modern science. Science is, after all, only "an orderly arrangement of what seem at the time to be facts." One M.I.T. physicist-turned-physician admitted to me: "There is not one thing in physics I am absolutely sure of." It is telling that modern physicists spend so much of their time pondering the uncertainty principle, chaos theory, indeterminism, and vacuum fluctuations. They can't even say for sure if Schrödinger's famous cat is dead or alive.[3]

In addition, scientists openly worry that we will never possess enough intelligence or technological sophistication to probe the final secrets of the atom or the universe. Observes Stanford's Roger Shepard: "We may be headed toward a situation where knowledge is too complicated to understand."[4] Some have called this point the ultimate scientific plateau — that point where not only our intellectual capacities are exceeded, but also our technological and financial resources.

Those scientists who wish to stay the course also discover

they must first become metaphysical mystics. Why is there such symmetry and design? How is it that the mathematics of the universe is so precise? Why is the subatomic world bizarre? How can a particle be a wave? Is there a "theory of everything"? Where did it all come from in the first place? Again, Hoyle complains: "I have always thought it curious that, while most scientists claim to eschew religion, it actually dominates their thoughts more than it does the clergy."[5]

THE ELEMENTAL ATOM

The word *atom* means "indivisible" in Greek. "The atoms struggle and are carried about in a void because of their dissimilarities . . . and as they are carried about, they collide and are bound together," wrote Democritus in the fifth century B.C.[6] For centuries, atoms were thought to represent the smallest unit of matter. This impression was in error, but *little* we did not know.

Atoms are indeed tiny structures. To illustrate:

- An atom compares to an orange in the same relative dimensions as the orange compares to the entire earth.
- To see an atom with our own eyes, we would have to shrink down to a billionth of an inch in height.
- To count the atoms in a drop of water would require every human on earth counting one atom per second for twenty thousand years.

Atoms form the basic units of chemical elements. There are ninety-two naturally occurring elements. Of these, eighty-one are stable, while eleven are radioactive, thus transforming themselves into other elements over time. The best-known radioactive element, uranium, is also the heaviest naturally occurring element, with an atomic number of 92.

Using particle accelerators, over twenty additional elements have been discovered. Such discoveries are difficult for many reasons, not the least of which is that the newer elements often have very short half-lives. For example, the latest element, with an atomic number of 118, has a half-life of one hundred-thousandth of a second, which explains why we don't find it lying around in train stations.

Hydrogen and helium are the two most commonly occurring elements. Together they make up the vast majority of matter in the universe, hydrogen predominating. But, for human purposes, the real action is with carbon (the fourth most common element in the universe). All known life forms are carbon-based. Carbon is the only element that has the flexible yet spectacular properties needed for supporting the richness of life. No other element can even begin to form the kind and variety of chemical bonds found with carbon. Using hydrogen, oxygen, nitrogen, and other elements, carbon can form an almost infinite number of compounds. We know, for example, of more than a million existing carbon compounds, many thousands of which are vital to life processes.[7] This property of carbon is unique among all the elements.

The story of carbon might seem common and earthy, but let me assure you—there is more than meets the casual eye. That carbon exists at all is either a cosmic freak accident or a miracle—depending on whether you prefer the odds of fluke or faith. Primitive carbon is formed when two elements combine. Sometimes combining elements is easy. But in the case of joining helium and beryllium, there is more involved. Combining these two elements to form carbon requires exacting conditions, and the chances of such conditions being met are infinitesimally small.

For one thing, this form of radioactive beryllium has a mean life of 10^{-16} seconds. Such beryllium brevity obviously does not grant the helium nucleus much of a chance to randomly bond with it. In order for the required bonding to happen, the resonance or excitation energies must be exactly mathematically matched—precisely what scientists have found.

When the math was first computed, unbelieving astrophysicists were spiritually stunned. "A delicate match between the energies of helium, the unstable beryllium and the resulting carbon allows the last to be created," explains Harvard astronomer

Robert Kirshner. "Without this process, we would not be here."[8] The carbon resonance match is both dramatic and extremely precise—and theologically suggestive. Hoyle was right: In plain view, Someone indeed rigged the physics.

For all of their special properties, each of the uncountable carbon atoms in the universe is identical. As described in previous chapters, our bodies continuously exhale air molecules, slough cells, and generally recycle cells and atoms—among which carbon is generously represented. Moment by moment we share our carbon life with the environment, other humans, and all other life forms. If we had some way of tagging our "former" carbon atoms, we would find them literally scattered around the world, under the sea, in plants and animals, and within the frames of all the people on earth. God, I believe, takes particular delight in creating meaning beneath the surface of the apparent. Thus the "cosmic religious feeling" that so entranced Einstein. We need only have "eyes that see."

There are other atomic elements that could be discussed, each playing a key role in the affairs of the universe or in the sustenance of life: elements such as phosphorus, unique in its ability to form energy-storing compounds; or oxygen and hydrogen, uniquely suited for the formation of the essential water molecule; or nitrogen, sodium, chloride, potassium, calcium, and iron, each essential in the physiologic processes regulating life. It is time, however, to shift our focus from the elements to the substructure of the atom itself. Here we have extraordinary findings awaiting us.

THE ATOM'S SHADOWY UNDERWORLD

When we think of the atom—if we think of it at all—we probably imagine it something like a miniature marble. But an atom is no more like a marble than cotton candy is like a bowling ball. When we put cotton candy in our mouth, it disappears. The same happens to the atom when we put it under scrutiny. "The physicist draws up an elaborate plan of the atom and then proceeds critically to erase each detail in turn," explains astrophysicist Arthur Eddington. "What is left is the atom of modern physics."[9]

An atom is a tiny puff of smoke that stays put. It is weaselly, ghostly, otherworldly. According to physicist Paul Davies, "Atoms and subatomic particles inhabit a shadowy world of half-existence."[10]

An atom is almost scary. If you don't understand what I mean, it is because you don't yet understand the true nature of the atom. It even unsettled Einstein, who, despite all his brilliant insights in theoretical physics, resisted the weirdness of atomic behavior as long as he could. Perhaps it is best to simply accept the fact that when things get this small, *the nature of reality itself changes*.

An atom is the original hyperactive kid. Everything associated with it is flying around like mad, bumping into things. The electron, for example, circles the nucleus of the atom billions of times in one millionth of a second. Subatomic particles are bursting in and out of existence as if they can't make up their nanosecond minds. A single oxygen molecule, comprised of two bonded atoms, experiences over three billion collisions every second. Very confusing hyperactive stuff. Atomic essence, looking for Ritalin.

Actually, it is this rapid movement that allows atoms to "appear" solid. Dimensions at the atomic level—just like dimensions at the astronomy level—are almost all occupied by seemingly empty space. Almost all of an atom's mass (99.9 percent) is located at its diminutive core nucleus. Yet the nucleus only occupies a hundred thousand billionth of the atom's volume (10^{-14}).[11]

The notion of the atom being the smallest unit of matter persisted until the early 1900s when British physicist Ernest Rutherford experimentally showed there were indeed smaller subatomic particles. Since that time, new particles just keep coming, like bedbugs jumping out of a moldy mattress. Every time a researcher hits the quantum mattress with a stick, out pops another quark. When the muon was first discovered in 1937, Nobel Prize–winning particle physicist Isidor Isaac Rabi greeted its arrival with a surprised, "Who ordered that?"[12] All the while, down in the orchestra pit the superstrings quartet plays "Ode to the Eerie."

Today, we know of over 200 subatomic particles, with the postulated-but-not-yet-proven superstrings representing the tiniest entity by far. The study of elementary particles is called particle physics or high-energy physics because the energies involved are enormous. Detailed lists of subatomic particles can get quite complex, and I see no need to go there. Let's discover what we can in the generalist mode, while leaving the complex specifics to physics classes.

The more classical view of subatomic structure is familiar to us all: the electron, proton, and neutron. This famous trio were the first subatomic particles discovered, in 1897, 1919, and 1932, respectively. While protons and neutrons are firmly stuck together in the nucleus, the electrons orbit around it in a manner more like a cloud than a ring.

Electrons—The electron spins around the nucleus so rapidly that the word "inconceivable" comes to mind. It has a very small mass, and a negative charge. Large numbers of electrons coursing through conductors constitute the familiar electric current.

Electrons move back and forth from an energy state to a particle state. This adds to the aura of mystery that surrounds their behavior and even their existence. If you look for a particle, you will find a particle. If you look for a wave, that is what you will find. "The 'inconceivable concept' of the electron as a 'wave of matter' touches upon a metaphysical dimension," observes Gerhard Staguhn, who writes popular essays about science and spirituality. "These 'waves of matter' are more than shape; they are metashape, shapes to which we can no longer attribute a substantial content—only a spiritual one."[13]

The behavior is so bizarre you almost have to suspend a "scientific" mind to even entertain the possibility, and then recalibrate your entire mechanistic paradigm to fully accept it. "The electrons orbiting each atomic nucleus obey weird rules," explains Berkeley professor and science author Timothy Ferris, "performing quantum leaps, for instance, which means disappearing from one spot and appearing at another without having traversed the space in between."[14]

Protons and neutrons—The proton and neutron both inhabit the dense high-energy nucleus, and unlike the electron, both are made up of smaller particles called quarks. Protons and neutrons are held together within the nucleus by a powerful bond called the *strong nuclear force.*

Protons have a positive charge. The number of protons in the nucleus equals the atomic number of that element (for example, hydrogen has an atomic number of 1, and uranium has an atomic number of 92).

Neutrons also live in the nucleus but have no electric charge. Together protons and neutrons, which have nearly identical mass, comprise almost all of the atomic weight of an element. Each is 1,836 times heavier than the ghostly electron. If you have the feeling you have heard *neutron* in an associated context before, you are correct. Neutron stars, for example, are hyperdense burned-out stars made up almost entirely of tightly compressed neutrons, weighing hundreds of millions of tons per teaspoon— thus rivaling the density of discount-priced fruitcake. Neutron bombs are a kind of atomic weapon noted for killing large numbers of people but causing less damage to property—perhaps the flipped effect of Hurricane Andrew.

The story of the atom, however, does not end with the proton, neutron, and electron. Beyond this more classical view of the atom lies a recently uncovered array of previously unsuspected critters, with more being added all the time. A few entries in this disparate tribe deserve mention:

Quarks—Perhaps the most notable category of particles is the quark, first predicted in 1964 and then actually discovered in 1968. Their whimsical sixties name was taken from a passage in James Joyce's *Finnegan's Wake.* Whimsy, however, did not end there. In all, twelve quarks have been named: up, down, charm, strange, top (or truth), and bottom (or beauty), plus their antiparticles. Protons consist of two up quarks and one down quark, while neutrons are made up of two down quarks and one up quark.

Quarks are tiny—a billion billionth of a meter. To do a size comparison, first enlarge an atom until it fills the distance from here to the moon. At that size, the nucleus of the atom would be as big as a golf course. A proton would be the size of a football field. And a quark would be the size of a golf ball.[15]

"Quarks" explains Staguhn, "are located in a physical 'somewhere' between matter and spirit."[16] Free quarks exist only in particle accelerators or at temperatures exceeding ten trillion degrees Kelvin. Such temperatures are not known to exist in the universe, thus keeping these particles structurally locked in a condition called "quark confinement."

Neutrinos — Neutrinos were first postulated in the 1930s and then discovered in 1956. Historically their name, given by Enrico Fermi and meaning "little neutral one" in Italian, is an off-shoot of neutron. Neutrinos are even more ghostly than the elusive electron. "Every second, sixty billion of them, mostly from the sun, pass through each square centimeter of your bodies (and of everything else)," explain researchers at the giant neutrino detector site in Japan. "But because they seldom interact with other particles, generally all sixty billion go through you without so much as nudging a single atom."[17]

A beam of neutrinos can pass through a trillion miles of solid lead and emerge totally unscathed. Produced in large numbers by nuclear reactions in stars, these numberless neutrinos — so vacuous that almost nothing can stop them — stream constantly across the universe at the speed of light.

For decades neutrinos were assumed to be without mass. Increasing evidence, however, suggests they do indeed have a slight mass, although so negligible it is almost impossible to measure. Recent studies indicate that perhaps the neutrino's mass is in the range of 0.03 to 0.1 eV. Don't worry about the units here — an eV probably means nothing to you. But take a look at the comparisons involved. Electrons, the lightest of all other sub-atomic particles, have a mass of 511,000 eV. Thus, if these recent calculations are borne out, the neutrino has only about one millionth the mass of an electron.[18]

Even though such a mass seems almost too small to bother with, it is nevertheless of great interest to scientists. For decades, astrophysicists have been looking for the missing mass of the universe predicted by their calculations. Neutrinos have infinitesimally small mass but exist in infinitely high numbers. When you do the math, it might indeed be the case that neutrinos are the answer to the "missing mass" puzzle.

The trillions of neutrinos that pass through our bodies every second come mostly from our own sun. After dashing through our anatomy, the landscape, and the earth itself, they streak out into space for a long, lonely journey to nowhere but the doorstep of God.

Photon—The photon is a particle of light. It was first advanced by Einstein in 1905, but initially resisted because light was considered a wave and not a particle. The existence of the photon was proven experimentally in 1915, and named in 1926 by physical chemist Gilbert Lewis.

Graviton—The graviton is a hypothetical particle of gravity. Such a carrier of gravitational force would function as photons do when they convey electromagnetism, and gluons when they convey the strong nuclear force. It is suspected but to date not experimentally verified.

Tachyon—Some scientists postulate the existence of a yet-undiscovered particle called the tachyon. If they exist, tachyons would inhabit a tachyon universe where everything *exceeds* the speed of light and nothing can be slowed to equal the speed of light. Einstein's relativity proves that nothing traveling slower than the speed of light can be accelerated through the "light barrier." But this theory does not preclude the possibility that particles might perhaps be created *already traveling faster than the speed of light*. If such a faster-than-light universe is ever discovered, tachyons would be noted to naturally travel backwards in time. Lacking any experimental data to support the tachyon's existence, however, most physicists are skeptical that they exist.

A few additional representative subatomic particles and categories of particles are included in Figure 3, in alphabetical order.

Figure 3—Additional representative subatomic particles and categories of particles

Boson — A boson is any particle that transmits the fundamental forces of nature back and forth between elementary particles. Included are the photon, gluon, W and Z particles, and the hypothetical graviton.

Fermion — The fermion is the basic constituent of atomic matter, such as protons, neutrons, electrons, leptons, and quarks. All fermions have a spin measured in half-numbers.

Gluon — The gluon is a carrier of the strong glue force that holds quarks together.

Hadron — Any particle made of quarks.

Lepton — A lepton is any of the six elementary particles and their antiparticles that are not quarks. These include electrons, muons, tauons, and neutrinos. They are not influenced by the strong nuclear force.

Muon — This particle is an electron that needs a diet, being essentially the same as an electron but 200 times heavier. One additional difference: the muon is also unstable, lasting only a few microseconds before decaying.

Pion — A pion is one of the particles responsible for the strong nuclear force bonding the nucleus together. It was first observed in cosmic rays in 1947. There are three varieties, each comprised of quarks.

Tau — Like the muon, this particle is a big brother to the electron. Whereas the muon is about 200 times heavier than an electron, a tau is 3,520 times heavier. It was discovered in 1974 and, like the muon, has a very brief half-life.

In an effort to discover yet more about mysterious particle physics, researchers are digging deeper and going faster than ever before. Particles at the Relativistic Heavy Ion Collider (RHIC), for example, are being accelerated to 99.995 percent of the speed of light. When these heavy ions slam into each other they are going so fast they don't notice the collision immediately. Instead they pass through each other and blow up an instant later—at temperatures of over a trillion degrees. Researchers are looking for a quark-gluon plasma, something never before observed.[19]

These experiments are so novel, so high-energy, and so unprecedented that they sparked multi-nation protests fearing the research-induced formation of a black hole, an expanding vacuum bubble, or "strange matter." Any one of these scenarios would lead to global annihilation, and possibly even the destruction of the entire universe! To pacify the worried, Brookhaven National Laboratories called together a distinguished panel of experts to investigate such possibilities. Their opinion, essentially "we seriously doubt it," gave a green light for the research to continue.[20]

ANTIMATTER

Antimatter is the most powerful substance known in the universe. Dramatic stuff, straight out of the pages of *Star Trek*. Yet it is real, not just science fiction. Antimatter was first postulated in 1929 by quantum physicist Paul Dirac and then first observed experimentally in 1932 by Carl Anderson, when he detected a positron.

Today scientists believe that every type of particle in the universe has a corresponding antiparticle: essentially the same particle but with its quantum properties (such as electric charge and magnetic moment) reversed. For example, Carlson's positron is the antiparticle of the electron. (It could also have been called an antielectron.) In the same way, every quark has a corresponding antiquark, every proton an antiproton, and so on. There even are antiatoms and antimolecules. In 1995, for the first time, antihydrogen was created.

Even though antimatter is a real phenomenon, it is not found naturally except in cosmic ray interactions. Its rarity is for a very good reason. Whenever a particle of matter comes into contact with its corresponding antimatter particle there is a tremendous explosion. Actually, annihilation is the more correct term. The annihilation that occurs when matter and antimatter collide represents the pure translation of matter into energy according to Einstein's formula $E = mc^2$. And the energy involved is huge! Upon annihilation with matter, antimatter offers the highest energy density of any material found on earth.[21]

Because of its explosive powers, antimatter is proposed as a possible fuel for space exploration. Penn State University has been diligently working on just such an application. Antimatter is so powerful that an amount equal to a shirt button would be enough to put the space shuttle into orbit. One proposal suggests that nine kilograms (about twenty pounds) of antimatter fuel could accelerate a one-ton payload to one-tenth the speed of light.

The biggest problem with antimatter is cost. At current rates, it costs about one billion dollars to create one milligram of antimatter. A second problem is storage. Penn State stores its supply in magnetic bottles. *Star Trek*, as usual, was ahead of its time. The Starship Enterprise used antimatter for its propulsion system in the form of frozen antihydrogen; it was always handled with magnetic fields and never allowed to touch normal matter.

When we think about the mysterious nature and awesome power of antimatter, let it remind us of a God who is greater by far than anything He creates. Does He ever play with antimatter? Perhaps using it to annihilate an entire galaxy on the far side of the universe, or making a throne out of it to impress the seraphim? Antimatter is both real and unimaginably explosive. As for the God who created it, the pillars of heaven can only tremble at His reproof and the mountains appropriately melt like wax in His presence.[22]

THE FOUR FORCES

Each bit of matter in the universe is influenced by four forces — no more, no less. Why four forces rather than two, or fifty? The simple answer is that God set it up that way and we have no idea why. Additionally, we also are in the dark when it comes to understanding why these forces work in the first place. We can measure them, monitor them, and manipulate them. But we have great trouble explaining them.

The four fundamental forces are the gravitational force, the electromagnetic force, the weak nuclear force, and the strong nuclear force. Each of these forces works with different strengths on different particles over vastly different distances. Yet if even a small change in the strength of one of these forces with respect to another were to occur, life as we know it would not be possible. Of the four, the strong nuclear force is the most powerful, and gravity is by far the weakest.

Gravity is the most familiar of the four forces and the first to be investigated scientifically. Even though it is the weakest of the four (more than a trillion trillion trillion times weaker than the strong nuclear force), it is nevertheless of massive importance because it controls the balance of power in the entire macroscopic universe. The secret of its success is the great range of distances over which it is effective. While the two nuclear forces exert their influence only within the tiny confines of the atom itself, the gravitational force extends to infinity. Gravity is, in fact, the dominant force of the universe at distances greater than the size of molecules.

Although Sir Isaac Newton clarified the law of gravity several hundred years ago, it remains a mysterious force. Think about it. If we drop a pencil, it falls to the floor. Why? Is there an invisible rubber band connecting the two? Obviously not. Why does the pencil drop? At the deepest level, we don't know. Yet if God were to suspend the law of gravity, we would need a steel cable six hundred miles in diameter to hold the moon in place.

One possible explanation for gravity is found in the theoretical gravitons. It is postulated that gravitons are tiny energy quanta that function within gravitational fields in a way similar to that of photons carrying light. But if so, how exactly do these gravitons constitute an attraction between the earth and the moon? We don't know. "We do not understand what mechanism generates mass in the basic building blocks of matter," observed the president of the Massachusetts Institute of Technology in 1995. Interpretation: we do not know why there is gravity.[23]

Another explanation for gravity is that it is not really a force like the others but instead results from the curvature of space-time in Einstein's general relativity theory. While this is satisfying in some respects, it still is not definitive.

One of the many strange implications of general relativity is that time and gravity are related. The higher we climb, the faster our watch runs. With every ten meters' increase in elevation, gravity weakens by 0.0003 percent, and a clock would run faster by one second in 100 million years.[24] While this effect might seem negligible in human dimensions, it is not negligible in the dimensions of our universe as a whole.

The round shape noticed in almost every heavenly body in the universe is another interesting consequence of gravity. Once something is larger than the size of an asteroid, the pull of gravity toward a common center crushes that object into the shape of a sphere. Reasoning from this basis, astrophysicist Hugh Ross explains that God evidently will suspend the law of gravity in forming the New Jerusalem. Revelation 21:16 describes this city as 1,400 miles wide, long, and high. Yet no such structure could exist within the pull of gravity as we know it, for anything exceeding 300 miles across would be collapsed into a sphere.[25]

Gravity is both kindergarten-simple and only-God-knows mysterious. "Gravity, like space, is ubiquitous and, like time, cannot be turned off," explains physics professor Hans C. von Baeyer. "Gravity passes through all materials, affects all matter equally, and has no opposing force, no shield, no antigravity. Only God can turn it on and off. . . . Inexorably it draws form out of chaos."[26]

In 1692 Newton wrote in a letter: "So then Gravity may put the Planets into Motion, but without the divine Power it could never put them into such a circulating motion as they have about the sun; and therefore, for this, as well as other Reasons, I am compelled to ascribe the Frame of the System to an intelligent Agent. . . . The Cause of Gravity is what I do not pretend to know."[27]

Electromagnetism is the other relatively familiar force. It provides electricity to power our technology and sparks lightning strikes during thunderstorms. It plays an essential role in human physiology—in cellular functioning, the bonding together of bones, the contraction of muscles, and even the testing of cardiac health by electrocardiogram. Electromagnetism is also the force involved with the orbiting of electrons, the charges of particles, and the binding together of molecules and chemical compounds. The streaming of photons and the photoelectric nature of light owe their existence to the same process.

This force was initially considered to be two separate forces using two separate sets of equations: electricity and magnetism. But in the 1870s James Clerk Maxwell discovered a set of equations that unified the two forces into one. This was the first successful attempt at unifying the various forces into one integrated whole, which ever since has become the elusive Holy Grail of physics: discovering the Grand Unified Theory.

Electromagnetism exceeds the power of gravity by more than a billion trillion quadrillion times. Yet the two forces are—and *must be*—precisely balanced for life to exist in our universe. A deviation by even 1 part in 10^{40} would spell catastrophe for both human life and stellar existence.

The weak nuclear force is, in some ways, more like an interaction than a force. It has a very limited range, essentially active only within the atom. Thus it is called a "contact force." It is the force responsible for the radioactive decay of elements like uranium. In the 1960s and 1970s mathematics equations were devised to link the weak force and electromagnetism into a single force called the electroweak interaction, bringing theoretical physics one step closer to a grand unified theory.

The strong nuclear force—another contact force—has an exceptionally short range of effectiveness extending only over a few subatomic particles. Yet it is incredibly powerful. It is the force that keeps the nucleus of the atom together. The nucleus, packed with protons all having a positive charge, would naturally want to repel each other. That such a repellent outward explosion does not happen is a tribute to the power of the strong nuclear force, which is about a hundred times stronger than the repelling electromagnetic force.

Any scientist first formulating an overarching unification of these forces would be faint with hysteria. To discover the grand unified theory (GUT) or the theory of everything (TOE) would bring worldwide fame and assure a Nobel Prize. It also would result in an immortalization similar to that enjoyed by Einstein's name. Yet such a discovery has proven elusive. Even Einstein himself searched the last twenty-five years of his life for this theory without success.

When British physicist Stephen Hawking was asked his opinion about the biggest unsolved problem in physics today, he did not equivocate: "The theory of everything. . . . We feel that we are near, but we never get there. It always seems just over the rainbow's edge." When asked if the task will be finished soon, Hawking replied: "My money is on it."[28]

Hawking's concluding paragraph in his best-selling *A Brief History of Time* reads: "If we do discover a complete theory, it should in time be understandable in broad principle by everyone, not just a few scientists. Then we shall all, philosophers, scientists, and just ordinary people, be able to take part in the discussion of the question of why it is that we and the universe exist. If we find the answer to that, it would be the ultimate triumph of human reason—for then we would know the mind of God."[29]

Hawking, who refers often to God in his writings, nevertheless does not believe in a personal deity or an afterlife. ("I believe that when I die, I die, and it will be finished."[30]) With such a brilliant and inquisitive mind, I would wish instead for Dr. Hawking the opportunity to sit for an eternity and discuss physics with the "mind of God" Himself.

FISSION AND FUSION

These four forces reveal to us that God has a power dimension to His creative abilities. Again, we do not know exactly why these forces exist—only that they do. God, however, has an intimate understanding of how they work and why they work. He could have created only two forces or two hundred. But for reasons known only to His own counsel, He decided to give the universe four.

As the human mind deepens its investigation of these forces we have learned to manipulate them. In so doing we have tapped into a vast universal power source that is almost infinite. (Science fiction writer Arthur C. Clarke predicts our new millennium will enjoy access to "infinite energy"—a concept that, because of fallenness, frightens me.) That we have access to such a resource should not make us haughty, for we created neither the force, the power, nor the energy. We are only using it—borrowing it from God, if you will. God has no objection. As a matter of fact, He wants us to use this power as a gift. But at the same time, we must always remain humble and realize He is the Giver. If we forget such a lesson, tears await us. When playing on a stack of dynamite it is always best to obey the rules and have a gentle heart.

This brings us to the rapidly escalating potential of unlimited power from nuclear fission and fusion. While neither one of these power sources yields as much pure energy as antimatter, nevertheless they are astronomically powerful. The tremendous release of energy in these two processes results from the binding energy of the nucleus and Einstein's famous $E = mc^2$. This equation, which we will explore further in the following chapter, reveals that a small amount of mass is equal to a very large amount of energy. The conversion, therefore, of mass to energy yields phenomenal and explosive energy levels.

Both fission and fusion sources are made possible because nature prefers the stability of mid-sized elements. The most efficient way to store mass energy in a nucleus is in the nuclei of iron. Therefore an essentially continuous gradient of energy storage efficiency exists from the lightest elements up to iron, and from the heaviest elements down to iron. Any process in which lighter nuclei can fuse or heavier nuclei can split is favored.[31] For this reason, the lightest element, hydrogen, is used in nuclear fusion, and the heaviest naturally occurring element, uranium, is used in nuclear fission.

Figure 4 — Gradient of energy storage efficiency		
(element, symbol, atomic number, atomic weight)		
Hydrogen $\Rightarrow$	Iron $\Leftarrow$	Uranium
(H, 1, 1.0079)	(Fe, 26, 55.847)	(U, 92, 238.03)

Fission was the process used in the first atomic bomb, developed in 1945, and has already been used commercially for decades. The release of energy in an atomic bomb is rapid, whereas the release of energy in a commercial nuclear reactor is dampened and controlled. Uranium-235 or plutonium is used in fission reactions.

The fission, or splitting, of this heavy uranium nucleus is accomplished by hitting it with a neutron. When the nucleus splits, it gives off two or three neutrons, each of which strikes another nucleus, giving off yet more neutrons. A chain reaction results. With every split, a small amount of mass is converted into a large amount of energy. The fission of every nucleus in one kilogram of Uranium-235 releases the same amount of energy as burning three million tons of coal.

Fusion is the process used in hydrogen bombs, first developed in 1952. These bombs are also called thermonuclear bombs because of the tremendous heat involved in the process. They are the most powerful explosive devices ever developed by humankind, prompting a gloomy Einstein to predict: "The next World War will be fought with stones."

The fuel used for fusion is hydrogen or occasionally helium—the two most common elements in the universe. When two hydrogen atoms fuse, the fused mass weighs less than the original two particles. Just as in the case with fission, the lost mass appears as energy.

Fusion is constantly occurring in the stars. This means that our sun is essentially a gigantic continuous hydrogen bomb. Every second it converts 650 million tons of hydrogen into 645 tons of helium, with the extra 5 million tons being converted into energy and released.

Figure 5—Comparison of Fission and Fusion	
Fission	**Fusion**
atomic (or nuclear) bomb	hydrogen (or thermonuclear) bomb
available now	not even close
uranium or plutonium fuel	hydrogen or helium fuel
fuel source limited	fuel source unlimited
less efficient	more efficient
significant radioactive waste	clean

The controlled use of fusion is technically very difficult to achieve, requiring extremely high temperatures. Any practical use of fusion as an energy source still appears to be decades away. Cynics have quipped that nuclear fusion is the energy source of the future—and it always will be. To date, the United States has spent over twenty-five billion dollars on fusion research without a successful harnessing of the process.

ON THE OTHER SIDE OF IMPOSSIBLE

Think for a moment about the kind of power God has buried within the nucleus. Through all the years of human existence we never expected the tremendous hoards He had stockpiled beneath $E = mc^2$, waiting for scientific man to discover what faith already knew. Think of the four forces He allows us to borrow for a season, seldom realizing there is even more if we but ask in faith. Think of the fleeting nanosecond subatomic particles discovered during the twentieth century. God knows each. Fleeting particles, but an enduring God. What is there not to believe or trust?

Although He lives in the land beyond comprehension, it is both comforting and frightening to realize that *He is not far from each one of us.*[32]

CHAPTER NINE

The NEW PHYSICS

SIR ISAAC NEWTON, a brilliant scientist and devout Christian, was born in 1642 and died 85 years later. His life and work changed the world of science as few had before him. Not until Einstein, 200 years later, would a similar force enter the world of physics.

Newton took the earlier work of Galileo and Kepler, co-invented the calculus system of mathematics, got hit on the head by an apple (probably not), and derived his law of universal gravitation. This law explained how the force downing the apple was the same force keeping planets in orbit and even ruling the entire universe.

Newton went on to propose his three laws of motion (Table 1). These laws established the foundations of classical mechanics that are taught in physics classes today, and also anchored what came to be called the Newtonian worldview. Science increasingly came to be understood as a mechanistic, lawful process. The concepts of physics — work, power, force, pressure, torque, energy, inertia, mass, motion, momentum, velocity, acceleration, heat, charge, current, field — were all reduced to equations. Life was predictable, mathematical.

Table 1 — Newton's Laws of Motion
FIRST LAW: The law of inertia
In the absence of outside forces, an object at rest will remain at rest and an object in motion will continue in motion in a straight line at constant speed until it is pushed to change its speed or direction.
SECOND LAW: The law of constant acceleration
If a force acts on an object, that object will accelerate in the direction of the force. The greater the force, the greater the acceleration.
THIRD LAW: The law of conservation of momentum
For every action there is an equal and opposite reaction. When one object pushes on another object, the second object pushes back by an equal amount.

Other laws followed, all binding on reality and constrictive of choice. The famous laws of thermodynamics (Table 2) arrived in the mid-1800s, summarizing the startling facts that energy is fixed (it cannot be created or destroyed), and increasing entropy is inevitable (the universe is running down). There were laws for electromagnetism, gases, optics, light, and waves. Everybody was getting a law named after him, while all the world was increasingly girdled by restrictive scientific fact.

By the end of the nineteenth century, however, a new band of prodigies began mischievously playing with theoretical dynamite, led by a young man named Albert. They scratched their precocious heads with one hand and wrote provocative theorems with the other. In the process they overturned Newton's apple cart, upset long-held scientific sensibilities, threw certainty into reverse, and exposed a startling mysticism in the universe. Now, instead of everything being fixed and certain, it looked like the entire universe was up for grabs.

This was the world of the new physics. It was not that Newton's order had passed away. But the new physics peeled back enough layers on the universe's onion to reveal that the less visible world—both the world of the very small and the world of the very large—was thoroughly weird. Before we explore this fascinating domain, however, let's linger within the classical paradigm to take a better look at the interesting first and second laws of thermodynamics. They have something to teach us about the creative sovereignty of God.

Table 2 — Laws of Thermodynamics
First law: The conservation of energy
Energy must be conserved between a system and its surroundings during any change. Energy cannot be created or destroyed. (Joule, Clausius, 1840s)
Second law: Entropy is increased
Heat will always flow "downhill," from an object having a higher temperature to an object having a lower temperature, thus increasing the entropy of the system. Entropy is the measure of the total disorder, randomness, or chaos of a system. The effect of increased entropy is increased disorder. (Clausius, 1850)
Third law: Perfect order at absolute zero
The entropy of a perfect crystal is zero at absolute zero of temperature. There is only one way of arranging atoms and molecules in a perfect crystal at absolute zero, and there is no process by which heat can be transferred out of the system at absolute zero. (Kelvin, 1851)

CONSERVATION OF ENERGY

FIRST LAW:
Energy cannot be created or destroyed.

When the law of energy conservation was first proposed in the mid-1800s, it was still fifty years before Einstein informed us that energy and matter were actually two forms of the same thing ($E = mc^2$). Today, however, we understand Einstein's principle, thus allowing us to comfortably expand the first law of thermodynamics to say that the total of *both* energy and matter are conserved. We can't make them; we can't get rid of them. We can move them around, transform them, or convert them from one form to another. But the total amount always stays the same.

This fundamental law teaches us important lessons about God's creative efforts. Scripture says that in the beginning, God created *ex nihilo*—out of nothing. He took nothing, and out of nothing He made something. When He stopped, creation itself froze in its tracks. No more. The universe became thermodynamically closed. In a very real sense, nothing more has since appeared or disappeared. Everything that changes is simply rearranging itself.

To explore the implications of this topic more closely, consider two questions: (1) How much mass-energy did God create out of nothing? (2) How much mass-energy have humans created out of nothing?

Question 1:
How much mass-energy did God create out of nothing?

In order to get a better handle on this first question, let's consider energy and matter separately. First, matter. How much *matter* did God create? The universe contains approximately 100 billion galaxies. In total, this is estimated to equal a trillion trillion trillion trillion tons of matter.[1]

Now let's consider how much energy this represents. Remember: to convert mass to energy, we multiply the mass by a very large number, namely the speed of light squared. In other words, another way of illustrating $E = mc^2$ is to say that a *small amount* of matter equals a *very, very large amount* of energy. For example, the tremendous destructive power of a nuclear explosion is the release of energy trapped inside a relatively small amount of matter.

The amount of matter God created in the universe is impressive. But the energy equivalent of this matter is much, much greater. And that is not all. Not all the energy in the universe exists in the form of matter. Much of it exists freely in the energy state rather than the matter state. Adding these two amounts together (the amount of energy existing within matter, plus the amount of energy existing in the energy state) yields an energy figure that is incomprehensibly large.

This is what God created, from nothing. And since that time of creation, nothing more has been added to it.

Now let's move to a second question:

Question 2:
*How much mass-energy have humans created
out of nothing?*

In all the laboratories, all the universities, all the military installations, by all the scientists with all their sophisticated, expensive equipment and Ph.D. degrees—how much mass-energy have they created out of nothing? Zero. Not one joule, not one gram.

For those keeping track of the score, it stands:

God → >>100,000,000,000 galaxies
Humans → Zero. Embarrassingly, not even a single atom.

For the unbelieving scientist, to explain how something as massive as the universe popped into being out of nothing is a formidable task. The most considered theory has to do with what is called a quantum fluctuation. This theory proposes that our universe exploded out of a dimensionless point called a singularity (with help from the zero energy point, virtual particles, Heisenberg's uncertainty principle, and the quantum vacuum—"a place so bizarre that it makes the Twilight Zone look like a clothing store"[2]). Yet how such a thing could happen is not well explained, because the singularity—although perhaps dimensionless—is still not "nothing."

We can summarize the first law and its implications by saying that in the beginning, God created a massive universe out of nothing; that since the creation event the total amount of energy + matter in the universe has been fixed; and that it lies beyond human ability for us to create even a small amount of either matter or energy out of nothing.

What does this teach us about God?

- That He is powerful at a level beyond human comprehension.

- That He alone has the ability to create mass-energy out of nothing.
- That He formed us with the ability to observe mass-energy—but not to create it.
- That if we need a source of energy, it is better to connect to God's energy source (infinite) than to humanity's energy source (nonexistent).

ENTROPY

SECOND LAW:
Entropy always increases.

The second law of thermodynamics is equally interesting, and again reveals something of spiritual importance. This law, known as the law of entropy, implies that the universe as a whole is irreversibly running down and cooling off. Even though the total amount of energy + matter in the universe is fixed, it always tends in the direction of increasing disorder.

In essence the law states that the universe flows irrevocably in the direction of hot → cold and order → chaos. Heat naturally dissipates. Order decays. All things naturally wear down. As order flows to disorder and heat flows to cold, the energy involved ceases to be available to perform work. Entropy is the name given to this overall quantity of unavailable energy.

The second law lies at the heart of all thermodynamics. Indeed, Einstein called it the premier law of all science. This law is not reversible. "It imprints upon the universe an arrow of time, pointing the way of unidirectional change," states physicist Paul Davies. With this law in hand, scientists have concluded that the universe is "engaged in a one-way slide toward a state of thermodynamic equilibrium."[3] This tendency will ultimately force the universe into a condition known as *heat death*, where its final temperature will be uniform and its final state will be chaos.

As with the first law, the second law also has theological implications. Because entropy flows only in one direction, we can trace both its history and its future. Going backward, we can deduce from the law of entropy that the universe had a beginning—a highly ordered beginning. If the universe had a beginning, how did it begin? And if the universe was highly ordered, where did this high level of order come from? Those questions are scientifically compelling, yet not answerable by science. The most reasonable and intuitive answer, of course, is that a beginning implies a Beginner, and order implies an Orderer.

Traveling forward into the future, on the other hand, we notice that such order is vanishing and the universe is on a one-way trip to the deep freeze. Why? Apparently God does not intend for this universe to be eternal. Our present home, it seems, is not to be the final domain of His creative effort. I am not implying that entropy is a reliable guide for dating the beginning and ending of the world. But I *am* implying that the law of entropy is theologically suggestive—it points to a beginning and an end, and thus to God.

The law of entropy leads to other important spiritual questions as well. For example, why did God create the universe with this entropic "bondage to decay"? In addition to the law of conservation of energy, why is there not a similar law for the conservation of *order,* or the conservation of *available* energy? God could have designed the laws of physics without requiring increasing entropy. For example, when we build an automobile, rather than it falling apart over time it could have remained stable at both the atomic and molecular level.

This tendency toward increasing entropy and disorder is reminiscent of the decay we associate with fallenness. If we build houses and don't expend energy to keep them maintained, the houses fall apart. Any order that we create will fall apart under the weight of the entropy law. We must live under the weight of entropy every day, just as we must live under the weight of fallenness every day. I am not necessarily asserting that the entropy of physics is synonymous with the fallenness of theology. But I am suggesting there is a connection. In a perfect world—a world without fallenness—I doubt we would be required to endure such a hefty burden of daily decay. I look forward to that eventual Time when both weights—the weight of entropy and the weight of fallenness—will be removed.

ENTER EINSTEIN'S RELATIVITY

In 1905, Einstein shook the world by the cranium, forever rearranging the synapses of science. Without warning, the undiscovered genius advanced from five sides at once, producing an intellectual earthquake of the first order.

Albert Einstein was born in Ulm, Germany, in 1879, and attended public school in Munich and later in Aarau, Switzerland. His disdain for the German military prompted him to relinquish his citizenship at age sixteen, although he did not become a Swiss citizen until ten years later. He graduated from the Federal Institute of Technology in Zurich in 1900, but was refused jobs in academic institutions throughout Europe. In addition, his marriage to an older physics classmate was not well accepted by his family on ethnic principles—she was Serbian.

In the five years following his graduation he was either unemployed or underemployed, and always poor. From 1902 to 1909 he worked as a patent examiner in Bern, Switzerland, a job that allowed him enough extra time to do physics in his off hours. An embattled loner working in obscurity, in 1905 he published five papers that redefined reality.[4] One of those papers, explaining the photoelectric effect by describing light as a stream of tiny particles called photons, won him the Nobel Prize in 1921 (the only paper of the five that Einstein himself called "revolutionary"). But it was his paper on the concept of relativity that most firmly secured his lasting reputation.

Actually, there were two major occasions when Einstein published on what has come to be known as relativity: special relativity in 1905 (easier to understand), and general relativity in 1915 (much harder to understand). Aspects of these theories are technical and mathematically sophisticated, yet we can summarize his findings in understandable language yielding startling truths about our world and the God who designed it.

Special relativity (1905) — This theory was the first of his two landmark relativity publications. In brief, this theory deals with the speed of light. *Special* here is used in the sense of "special, restricted case," and *relativity* refers to measuring phenomena relative to one another rather than measuring them absolutely. It should be noted that this theory produced perhaps the most famous equation in the world, $E = mc^2$.

In brief, special relativity holds — either directly or by implication — that:

- The speed of light is always the same for all observers.
- Nothing can travel faster than the speed of light.
- Time between two events is relative.
- Space-time is a continuum.
- Energy and mass are interchangeable according to the formula $E = mc^2$.

The fundamental postulate in this theory is that the speed of light is always the same for all observers. If a beam of light is directed at you, it travels 670 million mph. If you ran away from that light at 600 million mph, one would think that from your perspective the light beam would only appear to travel a speed of 70 million mph (670 - 600 = 70). Likewise, if you ran toward the light beam at 600 million mph, one would think that the light beam would appear to approach you at 1,270 million mph (670 + 600 = 1,270). Einstein, however, proved that the speed of light always remains the same regardless of how fast you travel toward it or away from it.

This is counterintuitive. But it holds true not only in the complicated mathematics involved but also by virtue of experimental measurements. For example, if I ran toward you at half the speed of light, during the time your watch elapses one second, my watch would elapse 1.1547 seconds.[5] This might seem a small difference. But as the speeds approach the speed of light, the effect of the difference approaches infinity.

General relativity (1915) — Einstein's second relativity theory, published ten years later, took the earlier more *specialized* postulates (special relativity) and *generalized* them (general relativity). In brief, this theory is about the geometry of space, and establishes a new perspective on gravity.

Special relativity dealt with velocity. General relativity goes beyond this to deal with acceleration. The proof involved is so difficult that it is beyond even the abilities of most highly trained scientists. Einstein asserted that gravity results from a curvature of space-time, thus launching the motto: "Matter makes space bend. Space tells matter how to move." In addition, general relativity also makes precise predictions about how gravity bends light.

The implications of relativity are confusing to normal thought and are abstractions to our usual dimensions of life. Yet the implications are indispensable for understanding the rules that govern the very large and very fast phenomena of the universe—especially light and gravity.

Many counterintuitive associations follow from Einstein's remarkable work, such as: energy and matter are different forms of the same thing; space and time are not separate entities but a single whole appropriately called space-time; light is both a wave and a particle.

Einstein was noted for his wit and humility. Not surprisingly, this aspect of his personality extended even to his discussions of relativity. "When you sit with a nice girl for two hours, you think it's only a minute," he famously quipped. "But when you sit on a hot stove for a minute, you think it's two hours. That's relativity." He was not only able to penetrate physics brilliantly, but his insights often ranged into philosophy and politics as well. In one instance, while at the Sorbonne in Paris, he predicted: "If my theory of relativity is proven correct, Germany will claim me as a German and France will declare that I am a citizen of the world. Should my theory prove untrue, France will say that I am a German and Germany will declare that I am a Jew."[6]

When he first returned to Germany in 1914 to teach in Berlin, he reassumed his German citizenship. The rise of Nazism, however, offended both his pacifist views and his Jewish identity. While away visiting England and the U. S. in 1933, the Nazi government seized all his belongings. This prompted his relocation to New Jersey where he lived in a humble home and worked at Princeton's new Institute for Advanced Study, a scholarly retreat largely created around him. He became an American citizen in 1940, and was instrumental in prompting President Roosevelt to begin a nuclear weapons program to counter the rising threat of Nazi weapons. Although offered the presidency of the fledgling state of Israel in 1952, he declined as unworthy of the honor. Albert Einstein died in Princeton in 1955.

Many of the implications of relativity seem almost spiritual in their essence—certainly mystical at the least. Understanding space-time as a continuum, for example, means that we can never locate the center of the universe (of course our cat knows otherwise).[7] What does God mean by that? Why is light such a central concept in physics? Does this at all tie in with God calling Himself light?[8] Why is there a "light barrier" at the speed of light? If an object were accelerated to the speed of light, its dimension would go to zero, its mass to infinity, and time would stand still. How in the world did God ever dream that up? How does this new-found relativity of time apply to our temporal existence versus the eternity to follow? Is God *in time* or *outside of time?* Did God invent time for our age or will there be time in heaven? If not, will there at least be sequence? Did God create time when He created matter and energy? How can energy and matter be two aspects of the same thing? How can space and time be a continuum? Are there other equivalencies that we don't yet know about?

The theory of relativity yielded important answers to the subtle workings of the universe. But it also spawned an entire new set of questions—many of which will be addressed more fully in Chapter 11. For those of us who always see God lurking in the shadows, the twinkle in His eye is unmistakable. What surprises will He have for inquisitive physicists next? Read on.

QUANTUM MECHANICS

As if Einstein's theories of relativity were not abstract, provocative, and counterintuitive enough, at the same time quantum mechanics made its debut. Also called quantum physics, this entirely new way of looking at the subatomic world was devised between 1900 and 1930 primarily by six men: Albert Einstein, Niels Bohr, Paul Dirac, Erwin Schrödinger, Max Planck, and Werner Heisenberg.[9] The word *quantum* comes from the discovery in 1900 by Planck that energy exists in small discrete bundles called quanta rather than in a continuous spectrum of arbitrary possibilities.

In essence, quantum mechanics deals with the world of the very small. If relativity is strange, quantum mechanics is thoroughly weird. When we enter the quantum world, reality literally alters beyond recognition. "Few if any people ever grasp quantum mechanics at a 'soulful' level," explains Columbia University's quantum field theorist Brian Greene. "The only thing we know with certainty is that quantum mechanics absolutely and unequivocally shows us that a number of basic concepts essential to our understanding of the familiar everyday world *fail to have any meaning* when our focus narrows to the microscopic realm."[10]

"I think I can safely say that nobody understands quantum mechanics," stated the late physicist Richard Feynman. "Do not keep saying to yourself, if you can possibly avoid it, 'But how can it be like that?' because you will go down the drain into a blind alley from which nobody has yet escaped. Nobody knows how it can be like that."[11]

John Polkinghorne, who had a distinguished career as a particle physicist at Cambridge University before becoming an Anglican priest in 1982, tells us that there were two great discoveries in physics in the twentieth century—special relativity and quantum mechanics. Of the two, Polkinghorne believes that the more revolutionary was quantum mechanics.[12] In comparing quantum theories to relativity, Feynman—who was one of the world's most noted practitioners of quantum mechanics—wrote, "There was a time when the newspapers said that only twelve men understood the theory of relativity. I do not believe there ever was such a time. There might have been a time when only one man did because he was the only guy who caught on, before he wrote his paper. But after people read the paper a lot of people understood the theory of relativity in one way or other, certainly more than twelve. On the other hand I think I can safely say that nobody understands quantum mechanics."[13]

It is tempting to believe that as we extend our thinking down to the quantum world of subatomic size we will find everything similar to our visible world, only smaller. In other words, the only difference would be one of dimension. Such, however, is not the case—not even close. Instead, as we descend into the quantum realm we find a completely different reality awaiting us. The dimensions are different, to be sure. But so is the very essence of particle behavior.

The first thing, therefore, that we must do is suspend the prejudice of our macro-perspective. Easier said than done. Even if we are willing to open up our thinking to a new reality, we still don't know exactly how to do it. And we are completely unprepared for just how much stretching the quantum world will subject us to. "Those who are not shocked when they first come across quantum theory cannot possibly have understood it," observed Danish physicist Niels Bohr.

"It is clear by now that *all* interpretations of quantum mechanics are to some extent crazy,"[14] explains cognitive scientist and consciousness expert David J. Chalmers. "Quantum mechanics gives us a remarkably successful calculus for predicting the results of empirical observations, but it is extraordinarily difficult to make sense of the picture of the world that it delivers. How could our world be the way it has to be, in order for the predictions of quantum mechanics to succeed? There is nothing even approaching a consensus on the answer to this question. Just as with consciousness, it often seems that *no* solution to the problem of quantum mechanics can be satisfactory."[15] Finally, Chalmers yields to an empiric approach: "Perhaps the dominant view among working physicists is that one simply should not ask what is going on in the real world, behind the quantum mechanical calculus. The calculus works, and that is that."[16]

What is it about quantum mechanics that elicits such unsettled responses from the scientific community, and that caused even Einstein himself to rebel against it? If summed up in a word, perhaps that word would be *indeterminism*. Let me attempt to illustrate. In our macro-world, a chair is a chair and a rock is a rock.

If you put the chair or the rock in a certain place, it would stay there. You could sit on them, and they would be solid. You could come back tomorrow and they would be the same as today.

But that chair and rock are made up of atoms and subatomic particles . . . and the atoms and subatomic particles do not behave themselves. This is, in essence, the problem. Atoms and subatomic particles are unpredictable. They will not stay put. If you come back tomorrow, you have no way of knowing where you will find them. If you tried to sit on them, you would discover they are a cloud of probabilities. If you tried to measure them, you would encounter uncertainty. "Every quantum bit has the potentiality to be here *and* there, now *and* then, a multiple capacity to act on the world," explain Oxford Brookes' Ian Marshall and Danah Zohar.[17] These particles are therefore not reliably at any one place at any given time. "The quantum world," explains science writer Ian Stewart, "is a swirling fog of probabilities, in which chance is a fundamental feature of existence, and where matter has a degree of fuzziness so that it may be doing several different things at the same time."[18]

Rarely can we say anything useful about the future behavior of a single quantum event. Therefore the words *unpredictability, indeterminism, chance, randomness,* and *uncertainty* all show up with significant frequency in the discussion of quantum mechanics. It is important to understand just how much these words represented heresy to classical physics. On a macroscopic scale where quantum effects are usually not noticeable, nature seems to conform to deterministic laws. But on an atomic level, uncertainty is indeed inherent in quantum systems.

Werner Heisenberg, a German physicist and patriarch of quantum theory, became famous by clarifying and quantifying one aspect of this indeterminism. The Heisenberg uncertainty principle explains that in the world of subatomic behavior, many of our measurements cannot be precisely known. Things we take for granted in our visible world simply do not hold in the quantum world. To the casual observer this might not seem to matter much. But for the classical physicist, this was awkward in the extreme.

In particular, uncertainty deals with paired sets of parameters known as *conjugate variables*—such as position and momentum, or energy and time. Basically the principle asserts that we cannot know each value of the pair precisely. Once we increase precision in one value, we force greater imprecision on the other value. This is not just a problem with our instruments; it is a reality within the quantum world itself. But in order to predict what is going to happen with these particles in the future it is essential to know *both* values precisely.

Let's take the case of the electron, perhaps the most used illustration for the uncertainty principle. We cannot know simultaneously both the electron's location and its velocity (more formally, its position and its momentum). The more we try to pin down the electron's location, the less we can know about its velocity. And the more we try to pin down its velocity, the less we can know about its location.

If we were to trap an electron in a box and then try to increasingly constrict its space until we could pinpoint both its velocity and location, we would find the electron getting more and more frantic, explains Greene, "bouncing off of the walls of the box with increasingly frenetic and unpredictable speed. Nature does not allow its constituents to be cornered."[19] We are therefore forced by nature into making a decision: which do we want to know precisely—the location or the velocity? We must choose, because it is impossible for us to know both precisely. "A certain amount of ignorance for the human observer is fundamentally built into the sub-microscopic world of quantum mechanics," explains astrophysicist Hugh Ross.[20]

As a consequence of this principle we can deduce that the universe is a very hyperactive place when examined on smaller and smaller distances and shorter and shorter time scales. "The uncertainty principle ensures that nothing is ever perfectly at rest," explains Greene. "All objects undergo quantum jitter, for if they didn't we would know where they were and how fast they were moving with complete precision, in violation of Heisenberg's dictum."[21] Such "quantum jitter" means that all borders are fuzzy. In lieu of precision, the best we can do under these new circumstances is construct probabilities.

Classical physics, however, preferred precision over probabilities. Actually, classical physics *insisted* on precision. It turns out that the universe was not listening, for despite objections the universe proved to be indeterministic at its most basic level. Newton's dream of a universal clockwork machine morphs in quantum physics to a universal roulette wheel or a game of dice.[22] Einstein, for one, was appalled. His initial unwillingness to accept this finding led to the well-known quip that God does not play dice with the universe. (To which his friend Niels Bohr retorted: "Einstein, stop telling God what to do."[23]) In disgust, he said he would "rather be a cobbler, or even an employee in a gambling house, than a physicist" if strict causality had to be abandoned.[24]

In the 1920s and 1930s spiritually minded people found the postulates of quantum mechanics theologically threatening. Today, however, almost all observers view the findings as instead theologically interesting. Quantum mechanics occupies the interface where physics and metaphysics meet. There are proven absolute limits on human knowledge, on our ability to measure, and on our ability to predict the future. The uncertainty associated with quantum functioning gives God an opportunity to intervene in history without blatantly revealing His activity. This allows new possibilities for the phenomena of miracles and answered prayer — possibilities that scientists can neither prove nor refute. It also opens a metaphysical door for the broader spiritual vistas of creation, providence, and free will.

Max Planck, one of the primary originators of quantum theory, was not spiritually shaken by its implications. Instead he maintained that both science and religion wage a "tireless battle against skepticism and dogmatism, against unbelief and superstition," with the goal: "toward God!"[25]

SUPERSTRINGS

Relativity and quantum mechanics both appeared in the first few decades of the twentieth century. Both were unsettling in their implications. Both required an entire recalibration of the scientific paradigm. Both were measurable and provable. Yet both, it seemed, could not be true. The theories collided with one another, appearing to be mutually exclusive.

This problem persisted for half a century until a possible reconciliation occurred with the arrival of superstrings. Within the theory of superstrings, general relativity and quantum mechanics not only tolerated each other, but they actually *required* each other. The irreconcilable conflict between quantum mechanics and general relativity's gravity was solved when superstrings not only supported quantum mechanics, but in doing so actually predicted gravity in a serendipitous unprecedented finding. For the first time, the world of the very small and the world of the very large could be conceptually merged.

Foremost string theorist Edward Witten of Princeton's Institute for Advanced Study (Einstein's abode) likes to call string theory a piece of twenty-first-century physics that dropped into the twentieth century by mistake. In its infant form, the theory was first postulated by Italian physicist Gabriele Veneziano in 1968. The theory then experienced only a low-level research interest among some scientists for over a decade until it enjoyed a resurgence of popularity from 1984 to 1986 (a period known as the "first superstring revolution") with the publication of more than a thousand research papers worldwide.

Superstrings are still theoretical. The theory is based upon staggeringly complex mathematical constructions, so complex that there are more than a hundred million possible solutions for the equations. Part of the reason strings are so difficult to comprehend is because of their diminutive size. If superstrings exist—and there is strong evidence they do—they are very, very small.

A superstring loop is a hundred million billion times smaller than the nucleus of an atom. To give a better idea of just how small superstrings are, let's compare them to other things more comprehensible. "Imagine, if you can, four things that have very different sizes," explains Freeman Dyson. "First, the entire visible universe. Second, the planet Earth. Third, the nucleus of an atom. Fourth, a superstring. The step in size from each of these things to the next is roughly the same."[26] Each entity is 10^{20} times smaller than the one that preceded it. To experimentally probe the domain of superstrings, engineers would have to construct a particle accelerator measuring one thousand light-years around. (A *light-year* is the distance light travels in one year—nearly six trillion miles. For reference, our solar system is one light-*day* around.)[27]

Strings are like ultra-thin vibrating rubber bands. It seems the entire universe is one huge disco, filled with infinitely tiny elastic filaments twisting and vibrating rhythmically. To better visualize what we are talking about, let's zoom the microscopic camera down past the molecules, past the atoms, past the electrons, neutrons, protons, and quarks. By now we have entered infinitesimal space, descending smaller, smaller, smaller . . . finally, we arrive at what first looks like a point. But as we approach closer, we see that this is not a point, but a wiggling string. According to this theory, the whole universe is made up of such strings.

This vibrating string has a surprise for us—extra dimensions. The visible world we inhabit seems to be made up of three spatial dimensions plus time. String theory, however, requires at least nine spatial dimensions, possibly more. These additional dimensions are tightly rolled up and thus not perceptibly applicable in the functioning of the universe.

There is much yet to learn about superstrings; many questions are yet unsolved. The theory stretches the human mind in unaccustomed ways. Whether we have the intelligence to probe at such a level of complexity remains to be seen. But what does it teach us of God? One important lesson is that He has created at deeper levels than previously known. How does He master detail at such size dimensions? Is there anything yet smaller than strings? Does He have all the strings in the universe counted? What does this say about His ability to monitor the macro-details of our individual lives?

More interesting is what the added dimensionality of superstrings tells us about the spatial realities of the spiritual world. If our visible world has three spatial dimensions plus time, and the superstring world has nine spatial dimensions plus at least one or two time dimensions, how many dimensions will we experience in Heaven? Apparently many more than we currently experience, with implications that are staggering to the imagination. For example, if we lived in one dimension, all we could do would be travel along a line. If limited to two dimensions, all we could do is travel on a surface like a tabletop. If three dimensions, we could travel anywhere on, above, or beneath the surface. What would it be like to travel in six dimensions? Eight? Ten? The imagination can scarcely go there.

God, however, lives there. And He is even now getting it ready for us. "Things beyond our seeing, things beyond our hearing, things beyond our imagining," wrote Paul. "All prepared by God for those who love him."[28] Personally, I can hardly wait.

AS THE HEAVENS ARE HIGHER THAN THE EARTH

"Whenever man tries to probe into the universe's dimension of time, he will finally be confronted with eternity," explains Gerhard Staguhn. "Where he tries to understand the dimension of space, he will be finally confronted with infinity. And where he tries to understand matter by separating it into ever smaller particles, he will always discover something that is even smaller, and be confronted with the fact that there is no final smallest particle."[29] These are discomforting answers for those who prefer certainty. Yet at the same time, this new reality is endlessly exciting for people who enjoy faith. It turns out that the universe is far more interesting than first suspected—scientifically as well as spiritually.

The challenge for us is to understand what the new physics teaches us about God. For one thing, it confirms that He is brilliant, a "superintellect." Additionally, quantum uncertainty shows us that He can never be pinned down. If we try to put Him in a box, He will vigorously refuse the experience. He is mysterious; as soon as we think we understand reality, He redefines it. Even as light is a central defining entity in the life of the universe, He *is* Light. He inhabits more dimensions than our imaginations can deliver; He manipulates time as it suits Him. He is unfathomable, just as He said.

Let the record show: God is impressive. But does He love us? Does He care? "Calvary is the measure of the love of God," says J. I. Packer. "Lay it to heart."

CHAPTER TEN

The STORY *of the* STARS

"HE who gazes at the stars unavoidably starts thinking," said Gerhard Staguhn.[1] There is something about the heavens that leads to thoughts of Heaven. Who hasn't had a quasi-spiritual experience watching the twinkling firmament with its shooting stars or northern lights? Or, while driving down the interstate, unexpectedly seeing a huge moon just cresting the horizon? But the best is just the night sky itself, rid of city lights, and with plenty of time to drink it in.

There is one sense in which the night sky is God's response to our questions and fears. "Lift your eyes and look to the heavens," wrote Isaiah. "Who created all these? He who brings out the starry host one by one, and calls them each by name. Because of his great power and mighty strength, not one of them is missing."[2]

When John Glenn had the opportunity to ride the space shuttle in 1998, he gazed once again from the unique vantage of orbit. "To look up out at this kind of creation and not believe in God is to me impossible," he remarked in an interview. "It just strengthens my faith."[3]

Newsweek columnist George Will wonders if the U.S.

government might be required to suspend the space program on the grounds that it violates the separation of church and state. "Soon the American Civil Liberties Union, or People for the American Way, or some similar faction of litigious secularism will file suit against NASA, charging that the Hubble Space Telescope unconstitutionally gives comfort to the religiously inclined," he jests. "Science . . . is augmenting, not subverting, the sense of awe that undergirds religious yearnings."[4]

THE UNIVERSE

In an earlier era, most scientists believed the universe was both infinite and eternal—meaning that it had no dimensions, no bounds, no beginning, and no end. Such a belief was appealing because it seemed spiritually neutral. Today, however, few scientists believe in an infinite, eternal universe. This has forced upon spiritual skeptics a First Cause discomfort they would rather have avoided.

If the universe had a beginning, where did the event happen? It is a question that surprisingly has no reference. When the universe began, simultaneously space itself began. Prior to such an event there was no space, at least that we can discern. And if there was no space, there was no "place in space" for creation to happen. The best we can say is that, consistent with the biblical record, it just happened. Additionally, although the universe seems to measure between ten and twenty billion light-years across, it is not possible for us to locate its center. We are floating somewhere in the middle of a pretty big cosmic bubble. Not to worry, for God has it all clearly marked with a gigantic pushpin in the map room of heaven.

The universe contains a trillion trillion trillion trillion tons of matter (10^{56} grams)—bringing a level of quantification to Solzhenitsyn's oft quoted Russian proverb: "A word of truth outweighs the universe." In addition, the observable universe contains a hundred million trillion trillion trillion trillion trillion trillion elementary particles (10^{80}). Not only does God know precisely where the earth is, but in fact He also knows precisely where each one of these subatomic particles is located. This might sound ridiculous to us: *There are far too many; they are too small; they move around too fast; and why would God be interested to track them anyway?* My response — stop thinking about God from a human perspective. Go to the dictionary and look up the word *omniscient*. If God is indeed omniscient, then He knows where each of these particles in the universe is located — every second of every day, for the complete duration of eternity.

To reach deeper levels of trust, we need to understand God correctly. To do this we need to approach Him on His own terms. Isaiah teaches us that no one can fathom God's understanding.[5] When we fully realize what *unfathomable* means as applied to His understanding, then it becomes easier to rest in His sovereignty.

When God set out to create a human-oriented universe, He apparently showed a preference for dimensional symmetry. The dimensions of the largest created entity — namely, the entire universe — are 10^{27} meters in size, while the dimensions of the smallest subatomic particle are 10^{-26} meters in size. Humans, at about one meter (10^0), fall precisely in the middle. When astrophysicist Joel Primack was asked about the significance of this, he was unsure. But, he commented, it does make for a "soul-satisfying cosmology."[6]

Some look at this vast expanse and feel overwhelmed by the puny insignificance of humanity. In Carl Sagan's movie *Contact*, Jodie Foster desperately searches for extraterrestrial life, saying repeatedly that if we were alone in the universe "it would be a terrible waste of space." Stephen Hawking likewise balks at the idea that somehow the entire universe might exist only for the sake of humanity. "The human race is so insignificant, I find it difficult to believe the whole universe is a necessary precondition for our existence. Clearly the solar system is necessary, and maybe our galaxy, but not a hundred billion other galaxies."[7] Nobel laureate physicist Steven Weinberg believes that religious experience "is an ordinary product of the brain," and that moral order is "created and imposed by us."[8] As for the universe? "The effort to understand the universe is one of the very few things that lifts human life a little above the level of farce, and gives it some of the grace of tragedy."[9] It's nice to be lifted above farce, but personally, I'd like the elevator to go a little higher than tragedy.

Others see the same universe yet have more hopeful conclusions. "As a religious person, I strongly sense . . . the presence and actions of a creative being far beyond myself and yet always personal and close by," says Nobel laureate physicist Charles Townes. Townes believes that scientific discoveries reveal "a universe that fits religious views"—specifically, that "somehow intelligence must have been involved in the laws of the universe."[10]

Similarly, noted astronomer Allan Sandage, who began his scientific journey as an atheist, was overwhelmed by the data to accept the existence of God. "It was my science that drove me to the conclusion that the world is much more complicated than can be explained by science," he says.[11] "We can't understand the universe in any clear way without the supernatural."[12]

God has, in fact, left clear evidence of His creative role in all universal artistry. "The world is charged with the grandeur of God," wrote the poet Gerard Manley Hopkins.[13] If we have trouble understanding the message of the firmament, it probably isn't God's fault.

THE GALAXIES

The universe is populated by galaxies. Our own galaxy is, of course, the Milky Way. But in addition to our humble collection of stars, the universe contains at least a hundred billion other galaxies. Each is peppered with about a hundred billion stars.

These galaxies are spread across the expanse of the universe, yet not evenly. In some areas there are Great Voids, regions containing few galaxies. In other areas, however, there are clusters of galaxies together, and even superclusters. The Great Wall, discovered in 1989, is the largest structure in the universe, with a huge concentration of galaxies. No one knows how or why it could have formed in the way that it did. Another area of note is called the Great Attractor. This mysterious region, only recently discovered, is so massive that it is pulling other regions rapidly toward it (including you and me, so have your cameras ready).

Perhaps a fitting illustration is to suggest that if the universe is your living room, the galaxies are like furniture, and stars are like dust on the furniture. The Great Wall is probably the largest sofa ever made. The Great Attractor is most likely a giant television screen in the corner.

Galaxies come in all shapes and sizes. "Galaxies are like people," observes astrophysicist Virginia Trimble. "When you get to know them they're never normal."[14] Most galaxies are either elliptical (shaped like a racetrack) or irregular (no distinct shape). The Milky Way galaxy is an example of a spiral galaxy, which make up only about 5 percent of all possible shapes. It is flat and round like a pancake. The spiral spins rapidly around the center nucleus like a pinwheel in a hurricane. Our earth, located on a distant arm of the spiral, spins rotationally at a half-million miles an hour.

Our galaxy is not classified as a great void, which is an existential relief. Instead, the Milky Way is a part of a small neighborhood—a cluster called the Local Group. Only a few of the galaxies in our Local Group are visible with the naked eye, including our closest neighbor, the Andromeda galaxy. The Andromeda galaxy is speeding toward us at 200 thousand miles per hour. Although a collision is not on the short-term calendar, it does bring up the question of what happens when galaxies fly into each other. In most instances the stars are spaced so far apart that head-on collisions are rare.

Our entire Local Group is speeding toward the Great Attractor at a million miles an hour. When we turn our attention in that direction, however, we can't see what the big deal is. Ninety percent of the cause of gravitational pull from the Great Attractor is invisible.

The invisibility problem of the Great Attractor is also a problem with the universe at large—namely, missing mass. In short, we are not sure where 90 percent of the mass of the universe is hiding. Because it is not visible, it has been labeled dark matter. Dark matter does not participate in the process of nuclear fusion that gives luminescence to stars. Thus, dark matter is invisible to our telescopes. Many theories are being actively pursued, but finding dark matter is like looking for a needle in a hay-universe.

THE STARS

Stars seem the centerpiece of the heavens. God determines the number of stars, reports the psalmist, and calls them each by name.[15] A star marked the place of the Christ child's birth. Paul instructs us to be blameless and pure, shining like stars in the universe.[16]

Lying on our backs at midnight on a clear, dark summer night can be awe-inspiring. The total number of stars in the universe is unknown, but appears to be between 10^{20} and 10^{24}. Yet with the unaided eye, we can see only a small fraction of even the stars in our own galaxy, and virtually nothing beyond that (except on occasion one or two neighboring galaxies so remote they appear as faint single stars).

Figure 6—Stars visible in the night sky	
(numbers rounded for symmetry)	
Downtown New York City	30
Urban	300
Rural	3,000
With binoculars	30,000
With a small telescope	3,000,000
With a large telescope	30,000,000,000

Some stars are very small—even smaller than our moon. Others are huge. The largest supergiants have a diameter of nearly a billion miles—a diameter that equals the orbit of Jupiter!

Interstellar distances are astronomical. Our closest neighboring sun, Alpha Centauri, is 4.3 light-years away. To give some perspective, if our sun were shrunk down to the size of a marble, Alpha Centauri would still be over 200 miles away. There is a good reason for these distances—namely collision avoidance. Since God did not see fit to equip us with a global airbag, He decided to widen the distances instead.

As mentioned in Chapter 8, stars are gigantic perpetual hydrogen bombs, generating both light and heat. Core temperatures can rise as high as forty million degrees centigrade. That stars shine by means of nuclear fusion was theorized by Hans Bethe in the 1930s, earning him a Nobel Prize four decades later.

Even though French philosopher Auguste Comte predicted in 1825 that we would never be able to discern the chemical composition of stars, we can now read them like a book. Using radio, infrared, ultraviolet, X-ray, and gamma-ray radiation plus additional techniques, we can detect the specific signature for each atomic component in a star.[17] It is easier for us to tell what is going on within a star than what is going on within our own earth's core. It is also perhaps easier for us to tell what is going on within a star than what is going on within our own heart. "One may understand the cosmos, but never the ego," observed G. K. Chesterton. "The self is more distant than any star."[18]

We have become proficient at reading the stars, but it is God who remains good at creating them. Because of His generosity, we receive life, warmth, and beauty from stars.

They are referred to in the first chapter of the Bible and the last chapter of the Bible.[19] A star announced His coming in redemption. Now, all who await His return say: "Come, bright Morning Star."

THE SUN

Our own personal star, the sun, in many respects is quite unremarkable. It is not very big, not particularly hot (as stars go)—in other words, perfect.

Our relationship with the sun is completely one-sided—it gives, and we take. Of course the sun has an almost inexhaustible energy supply from which to draw. Every second it converts five million tons of mass to energy and then doles out these rays freely to the universe. We intercept only one-billionth of this total solar energy output and yet that suffices for virtually all our needs.

- Ninety-nine percent of all the usable energy on Earth originates from the sun.[20]
- In one second the sun gives off more energy than all the people in history have "produced" during their entire stay on Earth.[21]

Like all stars, the sun's power plant is a continuously exploding nuclear fusion reaction. The energy from these explosions is released in the form of photons. Earthbound photons take eight minutes to reach the surface of our planet. Even though the amount of energy carried by each photon is tiny, trillions of them hit each square meter of Earth every second.

The core temperature of the sun is fifteen million degrees centigrade. It is so hot that a pinhead heated to the temperature of the center of the sun "would emit enough heat to kill anyone who ventured within a thousand miles of it," explained physicist Sir James Jeans.[22] The surface temperature is considerably cooler, a mere six thousand degrees centigrade. But as we go *above* the surface, to the sun's corona, the temperatures can rise again dramatically, to as high as one million degrees.

Even though the energy generated in its nuclear furnace is predictable day in and day out, nevertheless solar conditions change frequently. Within the layers of the sun's surface we can see all manner of unruly disturbances.

Sun spots are dark patches that appear on the surface of the sun, some of which can be seen from Earth with the naked eye. They were observed by the Chinese over two thousand years ago and were also well known to Galileo. Sun spots can be very large, even five times larger than the earth, and are caused by massive magnetic field fluctuations that cool areas of the sun. Sun spots phase dramatically in eleven-year cycles. When sun spots are frequent, it is possible to witness dozens of them in a group. A sun spot can develop and persist for periods ranging from hours to months.

Solar flares are the most violent events on the sun. These sudden explosive eruptions release the energy equivalent to millions of nuclear bombs. When sun spots increase, so do solar flares. When particularly active, they can be seen every few hours. When inactive, flares can be weeks apart. They typically last a few minutes, and during this brief time they can eject tremendous volumes of energy rays and charged particles into space.

Various solar disturbances and storms can affect not only the sun's surface but the entire solar system as well. A 1989 solar storm caused a province-wide blackout in Quebec. The same event melted coils in a transformer station in Salem, New Jersey, leading to a fire and a regional power outage. A more recent solar flare shot a gigantic magnetic cloud toward the earth. It measured *thirty million miles* in diameter and was moving *a million miles an hour!*

Whenever confronted by such facts, I ask myself questions about God. If we witness a magnetic cloud thirty million miles in diameter moving a million miles per hour—is God bigger than that? Can He move faster than that? If the center of the sun has temperatures of fifteen million degrees centigrade and pressures of seven trillion pounds per square inch—could God walk into the core of the sun, take a nap, and walk back out? Every impressive structure or event in the universe should remind us of a God who is greater than all His works. With a God this powerful, why do we doubt that He has the power to help us order our lives?

"There is nothing of a physical nature that is more friendly to man, or more necessary to his well-being, than the sun," said David E. Lilienthal, former chairman of the U. S. Atomic Energy Commission. "From the sun you and I get every bit of our energy, the chemical energy, energy that gives life and sustains life; that builds skyscrapers, and churches; that writes poems and symphonies."[23] All true. But the gift is not an anonymous one, for: "Back of the bread is the snowy flour; and back of the flour the mill. And back of the mill is the wheat and the shower, and the sun and the Father's will."[24]

THE PLANETS

Circling the sun in orderly fashion is a diverse array of planets, moons, asteroids, and dust. All planetary orbits except Pluto's are essentially flat with respect to each other, within seven degrees.[25] Each planet has its own characteristics, even personality. A few brief highlights may be of interest:

Venus (#2) is very much like the earth in size, density, and mass. Yet scarcely can it be considered a kindred spirit. Venus takes almost eight months to rotate once on its axis, making for some pretty long days. The rotation is in retrograde direction east-to-west, the only planet to do so. Venus's atmospheric pressure is ninety times that of Earth's. Low clouds of carbon dioxide and upper clouds dripping with sulfuric acid result in surface temperatures of nearly a thousand degrees Fahrenheit. Hurricane winds whip continuously around the planet, accompanied by repeated lightning strikes and deafening thunder. Not a prime honeymoon destination.

Earth (#3), the "blue planet," moves in orbit at seventy-two thousand miles per hour in order to complete its annual circle around the sun. A change in distance from the sun by a mere 2 percent would void our planet of life.[26] Earth's magnetic field (not all planets have magnetic fields) shields us from dangerous radiation, as most of the sun's charged atomic particles are deflected around the earth. Our moon has a diameter almost one-fourth that of the earth but only one-eightieth the mass. Its noon temperature is +200 degrees Fahrenheit and its midnight temperature is a frosty -200 degrees. If the moon did not exist, neither would we. The earth would rotate three times faster, subjecting us to continuous gale force winds. In addition, without the moon, the earth's axis would be catastrophically influenced by Jupiter's gravitational pull.[27]

In their recent book *Rare Earth: Why Complex Life Is Uncommon in the Universe*, geologist Peter Ward and astronomer Donald Brownlee do a reluctant dance with the miraculous odds, stopping just short of invoking the Divine. "It appears that we have been quite lucky," they write, explaining how the development of life on our hospitable planet required a "fortuitous assemblage" of the correct elements and "an intricate set of nearly irreproducible circumstances."[28]

"If some god-like being could be given the opportunity to plan a sequence of events with the express goal of duplicating our 'Garden of Eden,' that power would face a formidable task," they observe. "With the best intentions, but limited by natural laws and materials, it is unlikely that Earth could ever be truly replicated. Too many processes in its formation involved sheer luck." The conclusion: "It appears that Earth got it just right."[29]

Mars (#4), half the size of Earth, is not our closest neighbor—Venus is. Yet Mars has captured both our affection and imagination. It is the only planet that gives us a good view of its surface. Mars is called the "red planet" due to its rust-colored soil. For a century it was thought by many to have canals cutting across the surface, but the Mariner spacecraft in 1969 revealed these to be a chance alignment of large craters. Mars has two polar ice caps of frozen carbon dioxide, or "dry ice."

Jupiter (#5) is by far the largest of the planets. It is so immense that over one thousand Earths could be placed inside it. Because of its extraordinary speed of rotation—a day on Jupiter is only ten hours—surface winds are a thousand miles per hour. It has at least sixteen different moons, the largest named Io. Most interesting is the protection Jupiter affords planet Earth. Were Jupiter not positioned precisely so, comets would strike our planet a thousand times more frequently than they do.[30] If Earth is the quarterback, Jupiter is a giant offensive lineman, blocking everything in sight.

Saturn (#6) wins the beauty contest. Its seven individual rings, first discovered by Galileo in 1610, are not only glorious but gigantic. The rings are thin, flat, and detached. They average less than a few hundred yards thick and are composed of countless separate particles of all sizes. Saturn is second in size to Jupiter, 750 times the volume of Earth. Two of its many moons do a strange orbital dance. Once every four years their respective orbits intersect each other. Just before collision, however, the two moons actually switch orbits. If only Californians would learn to drive as courteously.

In his famous *Principia* of 1687—which Hawking called the most influential physics book ever written—Isaac Newton penned the simple phrase "Thus God arranged the planets at distances from the sun." Although very much ahead of his time in understanding the precision of planetary balance, Newton could hardly have guessed just how advanced that knowledge is in astrophysics today. Either the precision in our solar system and universe was preordained, or the human race won the yotta-lottery.[31] Either way, the facts force us to believe a miracle.

FROM BLACK HOLES TO QUASARS

Although it might seem that the fine-tuning alluded to above is specifically a matter of our solar system, such is not the case. The entire universe and all its various structures are participants in an engineering design accomplishment that staggers the imagination. Before we leave this chapter, let's become better acquainted with some of the more prominent players in God's architectural cosmic display.

Black holes are the stuff of science fiction and nightmares, of Alfred Hitchcock and *The Twilight Zone*. We are all fascinated with black holes but have no desire to meet one in a dark alley. "Abandon hope, all ye who enter here," was Dante's caution placed at the entrance of hell. According to Hawking, it is a sign that could also be appropriately placed at the entrance of a black hole.

No matter how mysterious or frightening black holes are, every galaxy has them. Our own Milky Way galaxy apparently has many of them. It is even possible that the number of black holes in the universe might be larger than the number of visible stars.

Where do black holes come from? Essentially they are burned-out imploded stars. Massive stars are torn by two opposing forces: fusion pushes out, while gravity pulls in. The perpetual hydrogen-bomb fusion reaction within the core of the star continuously blasts matter and energy outward; but the incredible mass of the star has the opposite effect, as gravitational forces continuously attempt to make the star collapse in on itself. When all of the fusion material is exhausted, there is nothing left to counteract gravity. The star implodes.

So far this does not sound very dramatic. The drama comes when we try to figure out when and how this implosion ends. The answer is: never. The star shrinks continuously, compacting its mass and greatly increasing its density. First, it implodes to one-half its original size, then one-tenth, then one-thousandth, then one-trillionth. According to Einstein's theory of general relativity, this star—like political reputations or movie stars' careers—can continue to exist forever in a state of permanent free fall without ever reaching the bottom. Such a state of permanent free fall is called a black hole.[32]

Because its collapsing density rapidly approaches infinity, the gravitational pull from this tiny dimensionless point is enormous. Anything that comes into the vicinity of a black hole will begin to feel the effects of its immense gravitational pull. There is a point of proximity to the black hole where it becomes impossible to escape. This is called the "event horizon"—where the escape velocity becomes greater than the speed of light. Once past the event horizon, everything is sucked inside as if by an enormous vacuum cleaner. Even photons of light are captured by it. Thus the name *black hole*.

Each object being pulled into the black hole suffers the same fate—inexorable compression down to a single point in space, and finally, to zero size. From this quantum nothingness, theoretical new universes can appear, and time itself ends. Some even speculate time can travel backwards within a black hole. "I don't think there's any question that a person could travel back in time while in a black hole," says Princeton physicist Richard Gott. "The question is whether he could ever emerge to brag about it."[33]

To bring some perspective, if our sun were to become a black hole it would first have to collapse its radius from the present 450 thousand miles down to 2 miles. A teaspoonful of such a compressed sun would weigh about as much as all of Mount Everest. To make a black hole out of the earth we would need to crush it into a sphere whose radius was less than one-half inch.[34]

Only stars one and a half times as massive as our sun are "eligible" to become black holes. If a star does not have sufficient mass, it cannot collapse with sufficient force to trigger the black hole phenomenon. When stars smaller than our sun burn out, for example, they collapse, but finally reach a stable size and become dense neutron stars.

If our sun were to become a black hole (it cannot — its mass is insufficient), the earth would not notice any change in gravitational pull. The sun or its resultant black hole would have essentially the same gravitational pull on us.[35] The most important difference we would notice is the total absence of light, which would prove fatal within a few days.

Although a small minority of scientists is still reluctant to believe in black holes, both theory and experimental evidence increasingly support their existence. There is good observational evidence from X-ray data and from the Hubble Space Telescope that there are mammoth black holes — with masses more than a million times that of the sun — in the centers of some galaxies.

Black holes are a mystical phenomenon in which, according to Clifford Pickover, "all the laws and properties of our physical universe shatter, where gravity turns time and space into subatomic putty, and God divides by zero."[36] Is God intimidated by them? Do you think God ever takes on a black hole, perhaps challenging it to a tug of war on a Sunday afternoon in Heaven? Can He stand inside the event horizon, taunting the black hole, and not get sucked in? A God who is that powerful certainly has enough majesty left over to help me get through the day.

Neutron stars are the smallest stars known. Our galaxy contains an estimated hundred million of them. Typically a neutron star has a diameter of only ten miles yet as much mass as our sun. Thus they are incredibly dense. A neutron star's interior consists of a material called neutronium, which is so dense that a thimbleful would weigh one hundred million tons. It is a hundred trillion times denser than ordinary matter.

Neutron stars form when burned-out stars (actually, exploding supernovas) collapse but do not have enough mass to become a black hole. Instead, the powerful nuclear forces within the star's atoms fight back—and win. The end result is their matter increasingly compresses until it becomes a hyperdense neutron star. The enormous densities within the neutron star are similar to those encountered in the nucleus of the atom. In essence, a neutron star is an atomic nucleus the size of a city.[37]

Pulsars are neutron stars that spin rapidly while emitting short regular "pulses" of radio waves. While a normal star rotates perhaps once a day or once a month (our own sun rotates about once a month), the hyperdense pulsars can rotate as much as 100 times a second. The bursts of radio waves—and in other cases visible light, X rays, and gamma radiation—are due to very powerful magnetic fields spinning with the star.

Magnetars are similar to pulsars but spinning faster—at least 200 times a second. In addition, their magnetic fields are 100 times larger than ordinary neutron stars (and a trillion times larger than our sun's), making them the largest known magnetic fields in the universe.[38] Magnetars, which are rare, were first theoretically proposed in 1992 and then observed in 1998. The forces emitting from magnetars can crack their metal crust open, causing tremendous "starquakes." If a magnetar were between us and the moon during such a starquake, it would instantly erase every cassette tape, ATM card, and hard drive on the planet. If closer, it would probably rip the iron atoms right out of our blood.[39]

Gamma ray bursts were first seen—by accident—in the 1960s by Air Force spy satellites, confounding astronomers. Gamma rays are the most energetic form of electromagnetic radiation, thousands of times more powerful than visible light. Gamma ray bursts (GRBs) were noted, at times, to be as bright as all the other stars in the universe combined—almost as if the Almighty were taking pictures using God-sized flashbulbs. These seemingly random flashes of intense high-energy radiation can release ten thousand times the total energy our sun will emit *over its entire lifetime.* The exact source of GRBs is still unknown, although astronomers suspect super-supernovae or mutually annihilating neutron stars.

Supernovas are tremendous explosions that destroy an entire star. After the eruption, the luminosity suddenly increases by millions or even billions of times over normal levels. This dramatic increase in brightness, which can outshine the entire home galaxy, will last for a few weeks and then slowly dim. The most famous supernova, recorded by Chinese and Korean observers in 1054, was bright enough to be seen during the day. The last supernova in our Milky Way galaxy occurred in 1604 and was observed by Kepler.

Quasars are rare distant entities that, when first discovered in the 1960s, were thought to be mysterious stars—thus the name *quasistellar*, later shortened to quasar. Instead of being nearby stars, however, these mysterious objects originate from the deep recesses of space and are moving away from us at rates approaching the speed of light. Quasars are extremely luminous at all wavelengths. They can be a thousand times brighter than entire galaxies, even though the galaxies are a hundred thousand times larger in size than the quasar. This intense brightness seems to emanate from the central core of the quasar. To explain such a high-energy phenomenon seemingly requires invoking exotic interpretations of Einstein's general relativity.

Nebulae are clouds of dust particles and gas. The name comes from the Latin word for "cloud." Diffuse nebulae are large collections of dust and gases, often containing enough material to form a hundred thousand stars.

Comets are small bodies with very eccentric elliptical orbits. As they approach their swing around the sun, frozen material vaporizes, forming a long tail of gas and dust. The tail of a comet is "about as close as you can get to nothing at all." If compressed, a cubic mile's worth of tail material would not even fill a shoebox.[40]

Asteroids are small planet-like bodies (also called *minor planets* or *planetoids*) that belong to our solar system. Known asteroids number in the thousands, although it has been estimated that probably millions of smaller asteroids exist that are less than the size of boulders. The largest known asteroid is about 600 miles in diameter. Most orbit in the asteroid belt between Mars and Jupiter. At least 300, however, have elliptical orbits that cross the orbit of Earth. By one estimate there are 1,500 Earth-crossing asteroids larger than a kilometer, and 135,000 Earth-crossing asteroids larger than 100 meters.[41]

Meteoroids, fragments of stony or metallic matter that pervade the solar system, are essentially asteroids on a collision course with Earth. Some have their own independent orbits around the sun; others travel in meteoroid swarms. Most are tiny and burn up upon entrance into Earth's atmosphere, whereupon they are called meteors or shooting stars. Others survive to strike the earth, whereupon they are called meteorites.

Cosmic dust also pervades the solar system. Tens of thousands of tons of cosmic dust strike the earth's atmosphere each year. Included are space diamonds—literal diamonds but only big enough to decorate bacteria, were they so inclined.

OF WORMHOLES AND WARP DRIVES

Ever since *Star Trek,* sci-fi dreamers have fantasized about space travel to distant reaches of the universe. With our current understanding of physics and present level of technology, however, such travel is impossible. At speeds of thirty-seven thousand miles per hour—the speed achieved by NASA's Voyager spacecraft as it left our solar system—even a trip to our nearest neighboring star would take eighty thousand years. It would thus appear we cannot even travel inside our own galaxy, let alone across the intergalactic universe.

Nevertheless, research continues. The discovery of relativity and quantum mechanics taught us that science, space, life, and the universe are stranger than we perceive them to be. It is therefore best to stay curious and open-minded.

Research into space travel takes many directions, but two of the most imaginative involve wormholes and warp drives. Wormholes are postulated shortcut tunnels through spacetime. No one knows for sure if wormholes exist. To date, none have been observed.

Theoretically, however, the possibility of wormholes originates from the theory of general relativity. In the 1930s, Einstein discovered that the equations of relativity allow a black hole to have two "ends" representing a bridge between two regions of space-time. This finding, however, was ignored by all but a few mathematicians until the 1980s.

Even though wormholes exist in theory, do they exist in reality? If so, are they microscopic or massive? Are they fleeting or persistent? Evidence suggests it would take an astronomical amount of precisely targeted energy to create a wormhole. Once created, wormholes would appear to be very unstable, easily disrupted by anyone or anything attempting to pass through.

While some scientists peck deeper into wormholes, others are looking into hyperdrives. NASA, for example, is investigating warp-drive possibilities that would allow faster-than-light travel. Here again, the work is purely theoretical and highly speculative. A University of Wales physicist named Miguel Alcubierre has proposed that a ship could exceed the speed of light by compressing space-time in front of it while expanding space-time behind it. To illustrate, if we were on a moving sidewalk our overall speed would be influenced by two factors: the speed at which we walked and the speed at which the sidewalk itself moved. In simplified language, this is how the Alcubierre's warp drive might function—not by propelling the spaceship itself, but by manipulating the space-time context through which the spaceship was moving.[42]

Only God Himself knows what will be the final verdict regarding wormholes, warp drives, faster-than-light speeds, hyperdrives, time warps, and parallel universes. Somehow I have a strange feeling that we have not heard the last from these mysteries of the cosmos. After all, it was the Almighty who first told us to expect things beyond our imagination.

A Reason to Trust

The universe is a vast, rich, and beautiful place. It is both comforting and fear-inspiring. Every molecule and every magnetar speak of God. "The universe," said Thomas Carlyle, "is but one vast symbol of God." All throughout Scripture we read how God forged His creation and then indelibly stamped it with His glory.

Partly the hand of God is seen through beauty. Aesthetic sensitivity and harmony were not necessarily a given. God *decided* on beauty. Sunsets and stars, northern lights and meteor showers, blue oceans and green forests . . . we should rightly be grateful that God ordained such elegance.

Partly the hand of God is seen through power—whether the extensive power of gravity that holds it all together; the concentrated power of nuclear fusion that fuels the stars and gives us life; or the awesome power of supernovas, quasars, and gamma ray bursts. "Sovereign LORD, you have made the heavens and the earth by your great power, " said Jeremiah. "Nothing is too hard for you."[43]

Partly the hand of God is seen through precision. There can be little doubt to any objective observer that the universe was indeed a behind-the-scenes, fully-manipulated "put up" job. Our planet's requirements for sustainable life were impossibly and narrowly defined from the beginning: not too much mass or too little mass; not too far from the sun or too close to the sun; not too far from Jupiter or too close to Jupiter. The gravitational force had to be precise. The number of stars in the universe had to be precise. "Scientists have identified 109 characteristics of our galaxy and solar system that require exquisite fine-tuning for life's existence and sustenance," explains astrophysicist Hugh Ross, "and that's to say nothing, yet, about the possibility of organic matter arising from inorganic."[44]

If He has displayed such lavish beauty, power, and precision, why do we have such difficulty resting in His sovereignty? The abundant witness of a created universe leaves no rational excuse for existential insecurity. If we have a problem with spiritual confidence, it is not from God's lack of revelation.

CHAPTER ELEVEN

TIME, SPACE, *and* LIGHT

ONE of these days, God will get up from the sitting room in Heaven, walk across the floor, and turn off the television set. When He does that, this present age will be over. Everything we know will disappear.

This is not to say that our present world is an illusion. In fact, it is very real. But there exists an even bigger, more impressive, more dominant reality. And when God says the word, that dominant reality will take over.

Our present world is real, but temporary. The more dominant world is also real, but permanent. It is infinite and everlasting. This is why the Scriptures so often refer to our present age as "temporal," and to the age to come as "eternal."

When God gives the signal, we will have some surprises in store for us. When He brings down the curtain on the final act, many of us will be stunned to discover what comes next. The new dominant reality will be so unfathomably different and strange that it will take getting used to. The Scriptures have hinted at what it might be like. But nothing can fully prepare us for what awaits us. It is impossible to stretch our imaginations that far.

"Now we see through a glass, darkly;" wrote Paul, "but then

face to face: now I know in part; but then shall I know even as also I am known."[1] When God says the final word, we will *see* and *know.* Things will no longer be obscure, uncertain, vague. Every question will have an answer. Every question mark will be erased.

If we want a sneak preview into this new reality, there are several possible ways to catch a glimpse. The Scriptures, of course, are the best way to envision the eternal. In addition, we can also benefit by a deeper understanding of the nature of time, space, and light. These three concepts have special properties. To be sure, they help define our present temporal world. Yet in a unique way, they also tether us to the eternal world. As we investigate them more fully, however, be prepared to have the moorings of your preconceptions loosened.

Einstein's relativity taught us that time, space, and light were not what we thought them to be. After relativity emerged, all of physics—even all of *reality*—was open for redefinition. Light, he explained, is not some smooth ubiquitous ray that fills a room, but rather a discrete quantum called a photon. Unbelievably, the photon travels at the same speed for all people in all frames of reference *no matter what.* In addition, once something accelerates to the speed of light, both space and time begin acting bizarrely. At the speed of light we witness several unearthly phenomena:

- Dimension shrinks to zero.
- Mass increases to infinity.
- Time stands still.

Time, space, light—let's examine each of these concepts and see if perhaps we might not be permitted a sneak preview into the physics of Heaven.

TIME

Time can seem boring. It is the one constant in an otherwise rapidly changing, increasingly cascading world. The seconds plod along, like the steady dripping of a leaky faucet. "Tomorrow, and tomorrow, and tomorrow," wrote Shakespeare, "creeps in this petty pace from day-to-day to the last syllable of recorded time."

Time moves only in one direction—forward. Aside from God Himself, no person or event has ever been able to change the direction of that flow. And it moves at the same pace for all people. Whether naked tribesmen in their Irian jungles or bespectacled professors in their Oxford classrooms—it makes no difference. Time is a resource we all share equally. Nobody gets a minute more or a minute less, no matter how we beg or bribe.

Time just *is*.

And then Einstein came along and threw the rulebook into the fire. Einstein proved that time only works in the usual way when we are comfortably in our routine frame of reference. Once we step out of that frame of reference, however, time changes. When in the larger universe—a universe of many frames of reference and great speeds—time warps dramatically.

By allowing us to glimpse this fact, I believe God is hinting at something. Through Einstein's relativity, He is allowing us a "sneak peek" revelation into the nature of Heaven. When God hints in such a way, it is usually worthwhile to follow His lead and try to discern His message. Following is a brief discussion of some spiritually relevant notions about time.

Time versus eternity—There are many theological opinions about God's exact relationship to time. The orthodox position— and my own belief—is that God stands outside of time. Time was a specific invention of His; in other words, time had a beginning. God created time when He created space and matter. When our age is over, God will un-invent time, and then eternity will take over.

Time dimensions—Time seems rigid to us because we exist in only one time dimension—a straight line. If we were able to perceive time as having two or more dimensions, many of our questions about God's miraculous powers would be easily answered. If God operates in more than one time dimension, it means that He can move around within our single time dimension and see everything happening simultaneously.

This is hard for us to perceive but not at all hard for God to do. We should never fall into the trap of thinking that if something is hard for us to imagine, it is therefore hard for God to do. A grasshopper has a hard time figuring out how a 747 works, but meanwhile the 747 flies overhead. Fortunately, the spiritual universe is neither obligated nor constrained by the meagerness of our comprehension.

Time dilation—The elasticity of time is not a spiritual apparition, but rather a proven fact of physics and an established observation in psychology. In physics we know that the elasticity of time is related to both velocity and gravity. The faster the velocity or the greater the gravity, the slower time passes. This effect is not simply an observational phenomenon. *It really happens.* It is called time dilation. The time dilation effect maximizes at the speed of light, when the passage of time stops altogether.

In psychology, time dilation is noted in the dream state. A dream of but a few minutes can, upon awakening, seem to have taken hours. Opium use can give the impression of an almost nonexistent passage of time.[2]

Musical scores and book plots— Works of music and literature are helpful illustrations to better envision how God stands above time. When we sit at a piano and spread out the music, we are, in a sense, acting like a person outside of time. It is possible for us to look at or play any portion of the score whenever we wish. We can also back up or skip forward whenever we wish. We can see the past, present, and future all at once.[3]

A book, perhaps a novel, also has several perspectives on time involved: there are the characters in the story, the author of the story, and the reader of the story. Time flows forward as the plot unfolds. Yet perhaps while writing the novel, the author took a break for a week, and then returned to writing again, picking up the story line at the exact moment in the plot where he left off a week before. Meanwhile the reader can begin at the front, middle, or end of the book. And once the reader has begun, it is possible to go back to the beginning and look at a passage again—thus, in a sense, going backward in time.[4]

Time and prayer—Many people balk at prayer because they can't get past the time issues involved. "How," they wonder, "can God listen to a million people praying all at once?" This is only a problem because of our dimensional blinders. Once these are removed, there are no obstacles left in physics or mathematics that would prevent God from hearing a million prayers simultaneously. As a matter of fact, God can listen to an infinite number of prayers at the same time, and take an infinite amount of time in answering each—all within the bounds of orthodoxy.

Foreknowledge versus free will—This problem, at least in my own view, is cleared up when we understand the extreme facility with which God operates within time. He lives in the past, the present, and the future all at the same time. "God does not 'foresee' you doing things tomorrow; He simply sees you doing them," explains C. S. Lewis, "because, though tomorrow is not yet there for you, it is for Him."[5]

God might know that something is going to happen to me next year—perhaps a car accident. But such knowledge does not mean He caused it to happen. He didn't *cause* it—He merely *sees* it. There is a difference.

If I act tomorrow out of my own free will, God already knows what that act is. To Him, being above and outside of all time dimensions, everything happens *now*. Yesterday happens now, today happens now, and tomorrow happens now. Just because He sees me act does not mean that He causes me to act.

Time and artificial barriers—That we can only travel in one dimension of time is an artifact, placed there at creation by God. The best way to explain this artificial time barrier is simply to say that God set it up that way and He must have had His reasons.

Another barrier that I believe to be artificial is the light barrier—the universal law of physics that prevents anything from traveling faster than the speed of light. I am interested to see what God will do with the light barrier in Heaven. Will He keep it intact? Or perhaps will He ordain that *every* frame of reference will somehow travel at the speed of light and thus never age?

Another possibility, should God choose it, involves three categories: when we want to go *forward in time* we will travel less than the speed of light; when we want to go *backward in time* we will travel faster than the speed of light; and when we want to be *stationary in time* we will travel equal to the speed of light.

When God eliminates the time, light, and speed barriers, it will be very interesting to see what kind of existence such a reality will afford us.

Life as a vapor—The Scriptures often refer to the brevity of life. James, for example, says that life is a "vapor" or a "mist": "You are a mist that appears for a little while and then vanishes."[6] In essence, what God is saying is that life is like a puff of steam. Throw a drop of water on a hot skillet, stand back, and watch. *Poof!* That, says God, is your life. I sometimes argue with God on this point. "God, I am a doctor. I went to medical school. I know about life and death. Life is not a vapor, it is seventy or eighty years." God replies: "Let's talk about it again in a billion years."

David then joins in the discussion, pointing out that our life is merely a "breath": "The span of my years is as nothing before you. Each man's life is but a breath."[7] Paul contributes as well by calling our afflictions "momentary": "For our light and momentary troubles are achieving for us an eternal glory that far outweighs them all."[8] "Momentary?" I ask God. "Why did You choose that word? These troubles seem anything but momentary. As a matter of fact, they seem interminable."

God replies, "I understand. But I am trying to tell you something about the temporary nature of suffering. I am doing this for your encouragement, to help you get through a fallen world. It might seem to you like a long struggle. But here is a secret: even though it feels to you that your perceptions about suffering are correct, in fact they are not. Troubles are momentary, fleeting, vaporous. You need only hang on for a vapor's length of time, and then you'll be Home. A vapor's length of time is not too long to do what's right. Trust Me."

In the following poem, for example, I am especially struck by the lines: "Pain in itself not hard to bear, But hard to bear so long." I don't know the circumstances that led to the writing of this poem. But whatever the circumstances, Faber's pain is now over. And from his new perspective, he understands why God used the phrase "momentary troubles."

"The Thought of God"

O Lord! I live always in pain,
My life's sad undersong,
Pain in itself not hard to bear,
But hard to bear so long.

Little sometimes weighs more than much,
When it has no relief;
A joyless life is worse to bear,
Than one of active grief.[9]

FREDERICK WILLIAM FABER (1814–63)

Time and Heaven—Exactly what God has in store for us we cannot know until Moving Day arrives. But whatever it is, it will be liberating. We will discover how dramatically we underestimated our newfound freedoms simply because our earthbound imaginations could never rise that high.

Even more, for the first time we will understand God's own radical power over the time dimension. When His mastery over time is fully displayed, we will wonder *what could have been* had we not so foolishly limited Him during our short stay on Earth.

It's About Time—
The distinction between past, present, and future is only an illusion, even if a stubborn one.[10]

ALBERT EINSTEIN

When God created time, he made plenty of it.[11]

IRISH PROVERB

Eternity is very long, especially near the end.[12]

WOODY ALLEN

Some people can stay longer in an hour than others can in a week.

WILLIAM DEAN HOWELLS

What, then, is time? If no one asks me, I know what it is. If I wish to explain what it is to him who asks me, I do not know.[13]

SAINT AUGUSTINE

When we've been there ten thousand years, bright shining as the sun, we've no less days to sing God's praise than when we first begun.

JOHN NEWTON

She was glad that the cosy house, and Pa and Ma and the firelight and the music, were now. They could not be forgotten, she thought, because now is now. It can never be a long time ago.[14]

LAURA INGALLS WILDER

Since God's time domain is more real than ours, it is more correct to say Christians shall all arrive in heaven at the same moment.[15]

LAMBERT DOLPHIN, JR.

High up in the North in the land called Svithjod, there stands a rock. It is a hundred miles high and a hundred miles wide. Once every thousand years a little bird comes to the rock to sharpen its beak. When the rock has thus been worn away, then a single day of eternity will have gone by.[16]

HENDRIK WILLEM VAN LOON

The shortest possible time is a New York minute. It is the time that elapses between a stoplight turning green and the cabby behind you honking his horn. That time is 0.00000000000000000000000000000000000000005 seconds. Physicists call this the Planck time.[17]

BERNARD J. LEIKIND

Life can only be understood backwards: but it must be lived forwards.

SØREN KIERKEGAARD

The English are not a very spiritual people. So they invented cricket to give them some idea of eternity.[18]

GEORGE BERNARD SHAW

With the Lord a day is like a thousand years, and a thousand years are like a day.

2 PETER 3:8

SPACE

Just as time was newly redefined by Einstein's relativity, so also was space. Space and time are inextricably linked. We can't have one without the other, and both are different than first thought.

It is easy to feel comfortable within the smallness of our three dimensional spatial understanding. The Newtonian view has scientific laws that work, and we have centuries of human experience to rely upon. But our comfort is an artificial one, for the topic of space is not nearly as simplistic as first perceived. We are therefore obligated to take a second look and attempt to understand what God's deeper reality is like.

Space and the void—When God created the universe, He called into being all that is, including all space, time, energy, and matter. When He spoke, the universe appeared. But exactly where in the void did it show up? *Nowhere.* And it continues to reside nowhere. He spoke the universe into being and suspended it in the void. If we attempted to send a letter to the universe, we would discover that it has no address.

Beyond the walls of our finite universe exists *nothing.* If we try to extend our understanding into this nothing, what is it like? Perhaps we envision it dark and cold like outer space. But *nothing* is not dark and cold, because dark and cold are *something* whereas the void is *nothing.* Dark and cold are properties of our own created universe. Such properties, however, end at the walls of our universe. Even the laws of physics exist only within the confines of our universe and do not extend into the void.

Nothing has no temperature, no luminosity, no energy, no matter, no time. And it has no spatial dimensions. This is not a *big nothing*, stretching for trillions of light-years. Neither is it a *small nothing*. It simply is a void. We could not take a spaceship to the far wall of our universe and then pass through the wall to continue our journey into the void. There is nothing to enter.

Even as we think about this, it is an overwhelming temptation to picture the void as having dimension. We picture our universe as a bubble suspended in a massive dark blackness. But this is inaccurate. The void is not massive, because that implies dimension—and the void has no dimension. The void is not dark, because it cannot possess the quality of darkness. Perhaps it is best to simply warn ourselves that we cannot imagine a picture of such a void because it has no reference in human experience. It is, by definition, the absence of everything. As we try to picture a void, we will inevitably fail because our picture will never be empty enough.

In the midst of this void—this nothing—God called out His creation. Our universe has temperature and luminosity. It has matter and energy. It has time and space. Specifically, it has dimensions—length, width, depth, and time. But length, width, depth, and time were all created, not preexistent.

In similar fashion, God called us out of the void as well. We exist only because He wills us to exist. "The Biblical teaching is that no creature has a principle of ongoing existence in itself apart from God's perpetual preservation," says pastor John Piper. "If God should ever cease to address your body and soul with the command 'Be!' you would cease to be. The only barrier between you and nothingness is the Word of God. . . . Apart from Him we fly into nothingness."[19]

Space and dimensionality—Our visible, temporal existence contains three spatial dimensions and one time dimension. In reality, these dimensions are not separate but integrated. Whenever we travel in space, we travel in time as well. We exist in space-time.

But are these four the only possible dimensions? Clearly not. God just happened to choose four functioning dimensions for us and not more—we don't know why. (In the same way, we do not know why God chose four forces. He seems to like the number four.) The powerful yet still theoretical superstring theory suggests there might actually be nine spatial dimensions, but God has hidden the extra dimensions from visibility by tightly coiling them into incredibly tiny vibrating strings. Other string theories incorporate more than twenty dimensions. This hints that the four dimensions so familiar to us are not the final verdict of eternity but rather an arbitrary condition God chose to use in the creation of this present universe.

God and dimensions—How many dimensions does God inhabit? The simple answer: as many as He wants. God is Spirit. As such He is non-physical and extra-dimensional. He has many options available to Him, among them:

- He can be dimensionless.
- He can inhabit a large number of dimensions, up to infinity.
- He can inhabit a smaller number of dimensions, as He wishes.

God can therefore be anywhere He wishes whenever He wishes. He can inhabit a human heart or an entire universe. He can be next to me suggesting thoughts, while at the same time helping a rice farmer in Vietnam and listening to a child's prayer in Argentina. Just because this might be difficult for us to imagine does not obligate God to conform to our limited paradigm. To better understand God, it is necessary to fully realize how He is differentiated from His space-time creation. If we can't first reach beyond our space-time preconceptions, stretching our thoughts up to the greatness of God will be impossible.

Space and miracles—When we understand how radically free God is from dimensionality, it is easy to believe in miracles, or even to *expect* miracles. For example, Jesus disappearing after visiting with the men on the road to Emmaus;[20] angels appearing and disappearing; Philip being transported away after baptizing the Ethiopian eunuch;[21] and Jesus walking on water.[22] These miracles are easy to explain once we introduce the possibility of operating in and manipulating multiple dimensions. Following His resurrection, for example, on two occasions separated by a week's time, Jesus appeared through locked doors to visit with the disciples.[23] "Jesus would have no problem passing through the walls of that locked room with His physical body," explains Hugh Ross, "if He were simply to rotate His body into extra dimensions of space."[24] Such thinking might sound like magic and fantasy, but it is instead consistent with sound mathematics and physics. (Which is not to suggest, of course, that God is bound by the laws of mathematics and physics.)

Space and the afterlife—The current creation, as wonderful and miraculous as it is, will one day end. When that happens, God will supply us with something far better. It is hard to know what kind of dimensionality this might entail, but it will include much more freedom of movement than we now enjoy. This might mean additional spatial dimensions and additional time dimensions as well. The result will be so spectacularly different from anything we currently know or experience that the comparison will make our present limited movement in three spatial dimensions and one time dimension (forward only) seem like shackles.

Space and relative size—When God created, He made some things much larger than our human experience and other things much smaller. In the midst of this range there is an apparent symmetry, as if we were the center point of His creation—which, of course, we are. While this is both interesting and satisfying, it is also instructive to point out that because we are locked into our own size experience, we are blind to much of the rest of creation. Things that are orders of magnitude different from our own frame of reference simply don't show up on the radar screen of our awareness. "We miss a great deal because we perceive only things on our own scale,"[25] explains *Los Angeles Times* science writer K. C. Cole. "Many times people argue about right and wrong when really what they're contesting is different reference frames. . . . Simply blowing up or shrinking down your reference frame can have enormous consequences."[26]

In his outrageously zany *The Hitchhiker's Guide to the Galaxy*, Douglas Adams introduces us to a weird consequence of dimensional scale difference. As the story goes, millennia ago two fiercely opposing leaders were sitting down at peace negotiations to avoid frightful interstellar battle. Meanwhile, far away in both time and space, earthling Arthur Dent uttered the phrase: "I seem to be having tremendous difficulty with my life-style." As he did, a freak wormhole opened up in the fabric of the space-time continuum, carrying his phrase back to the precise moment and location of the negotiations on the other side of the universe.

The vile warlords sat staring at each other in challenge, with "a million sleek and horribly beweaponed star cruisers poised to unleash electric death." At that precise inopportune moment, "the words *I seem to be having tremendous difficulty with my life-style* drifted across the conference table. Unfortunately, in the Vl'Hurg tongue this was the most dreadful insult imaginable, and there was nothing for it but to wage terrible war for centuries."

After most of their galaxy had been annihilated, the warring factions discovered that the battle was a big mistake, and they pinpointed Earth as the source of the offending remark. The remaining forces now joined together in alliance to destroy Dent, Earth, and the entire Milky Way.

"For thousands more years, the mighty ships tore across the empty wastes of space and finally dived screaming on to the first planet they came across—which happened to be the Earth—where due to a terrible miscalculation of scale the entire battle fleet was accidentally swallowed by a small dog."[27]

Along with his typical lunacy, Adams presents us with an important illustration. The specific dimensional measurements of our human existence have no cosmic, transcendent, or eternal significance. To be provocative about it, our entire universe might actually be but a tiny subatomic system within a molecule of God's throne. Remember—as we approach the speed of light, dimension goes to zero. How God will employ this fact in eternity is unclear, but the way He structures our afterlife will surely surprise and please us.

LIGHT

Light is the third entry in our time-space-light trilogy. What is there about light that caused God to show it such favoritism? He decided to single it out for special treatment and gave it properties unequaled in the universe. Even more startling: God equated Himself to light.

Nothing in the created order is equal to the remarkable essence God assigns to light.

- It establishes the speed limit for the entire universe.
- Its speed is the only constant in the universe.
- It is outside of time.
- It never ages.
- It anchors the laws of relativity.
- It is both a wave and particle.
- It allows us to see.
- It comforts us with its presence and depresses us by its absence.
- It conveys the energy and warmth that allow us to live.
- It consumes darkness but itself is never consumed by darkness.
- It is mentioned as the first thing God created after the heavens and the earth.
- It, apparently, has a divine aspect to its nature.

Light is such an ever-present aspect of life that, like all ubiquitous things, we take it for granted. Yet, if the truth be known, when in the presence of light we are bathed by a metaphysical uniqueness that is quite extraordinary.

A few centuries ago we thought of light as bright and warm, but there was no need to go much further than that. In the 1800s, however, light kept popping up center stage in theories and experiments by such luminaries as Faraday, Michelson, and Maxwell. Light was shown to be related to the electromagnetic force and to have a constant speed = c.

Einstein, therefore, had a historical background that contributed to his remarkable work, and other scientists deserve appropriate credit for their insights into the nature of light. Yet it fell to Einstein to put all the pieces of the puzzle together, which he so memorably did in 1905. His publications that year dealt extensively with the nature, properties, and characteristics of light. His paper on the photoelectric effect—establishing that light flows in discrete packets of energy called photons—later earned him the Nobel Prize.

The speed of light had already been established by Maxwell's equations as c = 186,000 miles per second. Einstein's work on relativity went further by saying that this speed always remained the same regardless of the frame of reference. Even if one star was moving *toward us* at 99.999 percent the speed of light while another star was moving *away from us* at 99.999 percent the speed of light, in both cases the light coming from the two stars would arrive at Earth traveling precisely the same speed—186,000 miles per second.

Furthermore, Einstein's work proved that nothing can exceed the speed of light. His equations revealed that as an object accelerates, its mass increases. As its speed finally reaches the speed of light, the mass of the object reaches infinity. Obviously, the object cannot go faster because it would not be able to exceed infinite mass. Out of the same equations came the equally startling result that time slows as speed increases. Finally, at the speed of light, time stops.

Light photons—The packets of light called photons are extraordinarily small. The familiar effect of visible light consists of large numbers of these tiny photons streaming out of energy sources. To better visualize what this might be like at the subatomic level, imagine viruses wielding machine guns that shoot staccato laser bullets nonstop. Even this image is hopelessly unrealistic, but it is perhaps a start in the right direction.

To give some idea of the number of photons contained in visible light, consider that:

- A flashlight with fresh batteries emits about a million trillion (10^{18}) photons each second.[28]

- A 100-watt light bulb emits about 200 million trillion (2×10^{20}) photons each second.[29]

Light as energy packets—In a remarkable engineering design, God decided to use photons as energy packets. For example, humans need an energy source in order to live, especially for food and warmth. God solved this problem by giving us the sun. In one long-term, slow-burn, nuclear-fusing, stable orb, we now had a source of luminescence, warmth, and enough energy to produce food.

But there was still one problem. Yes, we had a great source of energy—but it was ninety-three million miles away. How could God manage to get all that energy being produced within the sun across the solar system to His precious creation of planet Earth? The solution was typically ingenious—He would wrap each energy unit in one very tiny packet called a photon and then shoot these packets at high speeds in all directions. Earth would intercept a tiny fraction of the photons emitted from the sun (only one-billionth), yet this would turn out to be precisely the right amount to match our needs. To again demonstrate how small these packets are, every second about a trillion photons of light from the sun fall on every pinhead-sized area of Earth.[30]

Light and vision—Equally awe-inspiring is the design of the human eye. On the retina are over 100 million rods and cones. These rods and cones are photoreceptor cells that are light sensitive, converting images into electrical signals that can in turn be interpreted by the brain. The sensitivity of the retina's photoelectric cells is exceptional—as little as one to two photons of light can trigger a visual signal in each rod.

Ageless light—Because time stops at the speed of light, photons do not age. A photon that shot out from the sun and escaped into space a thousand years ago is still not even one second old. "Thus light does not get old," explains quantum physicist Brian Greene. "There is no passage of time at light speed."[31]

"At the speed of light (the highest speed attainable in our universe), time ceases to flow altogether. The time of all events becomes compressed into the present, an unending now. The laws of relativity have changed timeless existence from a theological claim to a physical reality,"[32] observes physicist and rabbinical scholar Gerald Schroeder. "Light, you see, is outside of time, a fact of nature proven in thousands of experiments at hundreds of universities. I don't pretend to understand how tomorrow and next year can exist simultaneously with today and yesterday. But at the speed of light they actually and rigorously do. Time does not pass. The biblical claim that the Creator, existing outside of time, knows the ending at its beginning is not because the future has already physically occurred within our realm of time, space, and matter. Einstein showed us, in the flow of light, the corollary of the Eternal Now: I was, I am, I will be."[33]

Exceeding the speed of light—Efforts are under way in some scientific circles to design faster-than-light communicators based on quantum connections. If they succeed, the intention is to use possible *superluminal quantum linkages* (theoretical and highly speculative) as a signaling medium.[34] I do not bring up such research to speculate about the possibility of its future success. Instead I want to point out that God already has provided us with a faster-than-light signaling medium—prayer.

We know that prayer originates somewhere in our brain-heart-spirit. But where is God's ear? One possibility is that God is so close, so omnipresent, that prayer does not travel at all. God intercepts it precisely as I am thinking it. But if prayer has to travel—even an inch—it must travel at infinite speed. Orthodoxy maintains, and I agree, that prayer is an instantaneous phenomenon. If travel is required, prayer must exceed the speed of light.

One additional spiritual property that travels faster than the speed of light is God's sight. Human eyesight is dependent on photons, which are bound by the light speed barrier. God, however, obviously uses a non-photon-based vision mechanism. We don't know how He sees—and we don't have to. It is enough to realize that He sees all things at all times instantaneously, and darkness cannot hide anything from His awareness.

Light and the spiritual realm—Everything about light suggests that it has a metaphysical dimension. Light regularly captured the hymn writers' imagination. As a result, the theme of light is a mainstay in the great hymns of the church.

> *Immortal, invisible, God only wise,*
> *In light inaccessible hid from our eyes,*
> *Most blessed, most glorious, the Ancient of Days,*
> *Almighty, victorious, Thy great name we praise.*
>
> *Great Father of glory, pure Father of light,*
> *Thine angels adore Thee, all veiling their sight;*
> *All praise we would render: O help us to see*
> *'Tis only the splendor of light hideth Thee.*[35]

Poetry with religious themes also deals frequently with the theme of light as a spiritual and hopeful entity:

> *Enthroned amid the radiant spheres,*
> *He glory like a garment wears;*
> *To form a robe of light divine,*
> *Ten thousand suns around Him shine.*[36]
> THOMAS BLACKLOCK

> *Sometimes a light surprises the Christian while he sings;*
> *It is the Lord, who rises with healing in His wings.*[37]
> WILLIAM COWPER

Throughout Scripture God refers to light in a spiritual context. Light is mentioned in the first chapter of the Old Testament:

> *And God said, "Let there be light," and there was light.*[38]

It is also prominently featured in the last chapter of the New Testament:

> *There will be no more night. They will not need*
> *the light of a lamp or the light of the sun,*
> *for the Lord God will give them light.*[39]

Light is always referred to in the context of hope and right-eousness. When God appears, a light signals the way. When God withdraws, the land is plunged into darkness. Jesus is heralded as the "true light," and then later says of Himself:

I am the light of the world.[40]

Most powerful of all light references are the passages where light is used to describe God's essence. In 1 John, God calls Himself *light*. Very seldom does God allow a noun to be substituted for His name. We do find it written that *God is love*, and that *God is Spirit*. But such occurrences are rare. In 1 John, however, we read:

God is light.[41]

Finally, the New Jerusalem, created as an eternal residence for the redeemed, is marked by two notable absences: no temple and no sun. In a tremendous display of glory and holy splendor, the Lord God Almighty and the Lamb are both the temple and the light of the Holy City:

The city does not need the sun or the moon to shine on it,
for the glory of God gives it light, and the Lamb is its
lamp. The nations will walk by its light, and the kings
of the earth will bring their splendor into it.
On no day will its gates ever be shut,
for there will be no night there.[42]

What will it be like to someday have God, the Great Physicist, take over? He will redefine everything, change the laws of science, and rid His realm of decay, pain, and aging. He will introduce new dimensions that will grant us mobility and communication pos-sibilities previously unimagined.

And in our midst will be a Light so brilliant that it would blind us with fear had it not first swallowed us with Love.

CHAPTER TWELVE

SCIENCE, SCRIPTURE, *and* SOVEREIGNTY

SCIENCE has much to teach us about the power and precision of God. Scripture points in the same direction. Both reveal that God's strength is impressive, His wisdom is unfathomable, and His rule is sovereign.

Even though God discloses Himself both in science and Scripture, still much mystery remains. Partly this is because our finite understanding can never fully penetrate His infinite reality, no matter how advanced or sophisticated we become.

But there is another explanation for mystery besides unfathomability, namely that God conceals from us vast stretches of ultimate reality. It is like the summit of Mount McKinley—we know it is up there but seldom see it through the clouds.

As the centuries and millennia pass, however, God slowly pulls back the curtain and opens up the door. Even though many mysteries remain, through ancient scriptural revelation and recent scientific discovery, the Creator has allowed us to see new spiritual truths and scientific principles that demonstrate His nature. As the "glass darkly" lightens, our understanding of the greatness of God deepens.

JESUS REVEALED

Let's rewind the videotape four thousand years, back to a time when people knew little about God. The Almighty, shrouded in mystery, called Abram's name and led him to a new land. As a result, Abraham knew more about God than those before him. Moses heard God speak in a burning bush, witnessed the miracles of the plagues, received the commandments, felt the mountain tremble, and saw God's glory. Then he wrote it all down, and we began to understand God better: that He was awesome and righteous, that He was concerned with justice, and that He loved us.

Four hundred years later, God promised David an eternal kingdom, and the plan of a messiah began to emerge out of the mystery surrounding God. A millennium passed. Then, in the greatest unveiling of mystery since Creation, a baby was born. That event changed everything.

With the birth of Christ, God now lived and breathed in our midst, walked and worked at our side. But even this Jesus was often mysterious, speaking in cryptic parables and telling His disciples "The knowledge of the secrets of the kingdom of heaven has been given to you, but not to them."[1]

Yet it was impossible to conceal that there was something different about this Man. By allowing the world to see Jesus directly, God opened wide a window. Now we could glimpse all the way into the eternal. Those who surrounded Christ experienced His words and power firsthand: seeing His miracles, hearing His wisdom, feeling His compassion.

We, of course, were not there. But God made provision for us to listen in. Through the Gospels we read that the people were filled with awe. "A great prophet has appeared among us," they said. "God has come to help his people."[2] The crowds were amazed by His miracles and said, "Nothing like this has ever been seen in Israel."[3] People were overwhelmed, saying "He has done everything well. . . . He even makes the deaf hear and the mute speak."[4] After another healing, the people were so amazed that they asked each other, "What is this? A new teaching — and with authority! He even gives orders to evil spirits and they obey him."[5] Following each miraculous healing, we read that the people were "amazed at the greatness of God," saying such things as "We have never seen anything like this!" and "We have seen remarkable things today."[6]

A teacher of the law was overheard telling Jesus, "Teacher, I will follow you wherever you go."[7] Peter, after one of the miracles, fell at Jesus' knees and said, "Go away from me, Lord; I am a sinful man!"[8] When Nathanael saw Jesus, he declared, "Rabbi, you are the Son of God; you are the King of Israel."[9] When John the Baptist saw Jesus, he said, "Look, the Lamb of God, who takes away the sin of the world!"[10]

The Pharisees said to one another, "Look how the whole world has gone after him!"[11] In fear and amazement the disciples asked one another, "Who is this? He commands even the winds and the water, and they obey him."[12] Peter came and told Him, "Everyone is looking for you!"[13] When the disciples saw Him walking on the lake, they were terrified. "It's a ghost," they cried out in fear. A few minutes later, when He climbed into the boat, the disciples exclaimed, "Truly you are the Son of God."[14]

When He was a child in the temple, everyone who heard Him was amazed at His understanding and His answers.[15] The Jews were astonished and asked, "How did this man get such learning without having studied?"[16] Teaching in the temple courts, "the large crowd listened to him with delight."[17] The crowds at the Mount of Beatitudes were amazed at His teaching because He taught as one who had authority, and not as their teachers of the law.[18] Later, reading in the synagogue, all eyes were fastened on Him. All spoke well of Him and were amazed at the gracious words that came from His lips.[19]

The woman at the well went back to town and said to the people, "Come, see a man who told me everything I ever did. Could this be the Christ?" The townspeople later said to the woman, "We no longer believe just because of what you said; now we have heard for ourselves, and we know that this man really is the Savior of the world."[20]

As He entered Jerusalem, the people laid down palm leaves

and exclaimed, "Hosanna! Blessed is he who comes in the name of the Lord!"[21] The temple guards sent to capture Jesus returned emptyhanded, saying, "No one ever spoke the way this man does."[22] When Herod saw Jesus, he was greatly pleased, because for a long time he had been wanting to see Him. From what he had heard about Him, Herod hoped to see Him perform a miracle.[23] At His crucifixion, when the centurion heard His cry and saw how He died, he said, "Surely this man was the Son of God!"[24] After His resurrection, the two men on the road to Emmaus asked each other, "Were not our hearts burning within us while he talked with us on the road and opened the Scriptures to us?"[25]

Those who walked with Christ were consistently amazed and overwhelmed. Their hearts burned. It was surely an incomparable experience. Here was powerful, almost irresistible, evidence of the nature of God—a deity who could cure illness, conquer death, and rule time, space, and matter. He was unjustly accused, wrongly condemned, and brutally crucified. Yet when He climbed back out of the grave, He wasn't even mad! What kind of messiah was this? He was, said Malcolm Muggeridge, the kind of messiah who ruled from the cross and whose only power was sacrificial love.[26]

SCIENCE REVEALED

The people who lived at the time of Christ enjoyed a special privilege: they looked God in the eye. While we do not have that physical proximity to Jesus, we have one advantage earlier people lacked: the new discoveries of science. While science hardly compares to the physical presence of Jesus or the revealed truth of Scripture, we would be wise to not underestimate it. It provides us an advantage in spiritual perspective previous generations could hardly imagine.

People of faith often tend to fear science or even dread it. My feeling, however, is quite different. Science is thrilling. True science is a friend of Truth. It is only the misinterpretation and misapplication of science that ought be feared (and yes, feared greatly). Truthful science, however, always tells us much about the power, precision, design, and sovereignty of God—details we learn nowhere else.

God has allowed us the privilege of living in a time when great mysteries are being uncovered. No previous era knew about quantum mechanics, relativity, subatomic particles, supernovas, ageless photons, or DNA. They all reveal the stunning genius of a God who spoke a time-space-matter-light universe into existence, balanced it with impossible requirements of precision, and then gifted it with life.

Does it not stir your heart to realize that in a millionth of a second, a trillion atoms in your body turn over—and yet somehow God makes it work? Does it not deepen your reverence to realize that God is more impressive than a magnetic cloud thirty million miles in diameter careening through space at a million miles an hour, or a neutron star that weighs hundreds of millions of tons per teaspoon?

Does it not give you pause to think that of the ten thousand trillion (10^{16}) words spoken by humans since the dawn of time, God heard every one, remembers every one, can recite them all backwards from memory, and even knew them before they were spoken? Or that of the 10^{30} snow crystals necessary to form an Ice Age, each snowflake—comprised of a hundred million trillion water molecules—is unique in all the universe?[27] A British mathematician has determined that the precision seen in the created universe is on the order of $10^{10^{123}}$.[28] How can that fail to impress? Science is a close friend of the theology of sovereignty. None of these findings were understood in detail until science uncovered them. When science digs, faith rightly grows.

SOVEREIGNTY AND THE REST OF OUR LIVES

The truths of Scripture, the life of Christ, the discoveries of science—all should combine to lift us heavenward. Yet we remain strangely anxious. Our days are swamped by the mundane; our nights are swallowed by insomnia. Seldom do we know true restedness. Yet God would tell us, "Be still before me; wait patiently. Trust in me, and I will give you rest."

We know that God is out there, that He sees and cares. But we are still tempted to run our lives independently, often consulting Him only for crises or trivialities. Yet God would tell us, "Don't you know that I care more about you than a hundred billion galaxies? That I work in your life on a thousand levels all at the same time?"

We have heard that God is strong, but perhaps have trouble believing that His strength extends all the way to *our* problems. "Most of us believe God can move mountains," observes Russ Johnston. "But how many of us believe He will? There's a world of difference. We believe God can work mightily on our behalf, but we really aren't sure He will."[29] Yet God would tell us if we but "have faith as a grain of mustard seed . . ."[30]

The Almighty has sufficiently demonstrated His greatness in both the Scriptures and science. The problem is not a deficiency on God's part but rather a dimness on ours. "Spirit of God descend upon my heart . . . I ask no dreams, no prophet ecstasies . . . but take the dimness of my soul away."[31] Only then will we rest under a full awareness of His dominion. "Oh, that we might learn the undefeatedness of God!" said Watchman Nee.

In the end, sovereignty wins. In the end, glory will be unrestrained. Finally, at long last, God will deliver us from our dimness. And in the shelter of the Most High, we will enter our rest.

Notes

Introduction: A New Vision of Power

1. Annie Dillard, *Teaching a Stone to Talk: Expeditions and Encounters* (New York: HarperPerennial, 1982), page 52.
2. Shirley A. Jones (editor), quoting George Washington Carver, *The Mind of God & Other Musings: The Wisdom of Science* (San Rafael, CA: New World Library, 1994), page 56.
3. "Reflections," quoting Thomas Merton from a 1965 audiotape, *Christianity Today,* 11 January 1999, page 80.
4. Jack Stimmel, quoting Charles Spurgeon, "Heaven's Song—Earth's Only Hope," sermon delivered in Menomonie, WI, 11 April 1999.
5. K. C. Cole, quoting Sir James Jeans, *The Universe and the Teacup: The Mathematics of Truth and Beauty* (San Diego: Harcourt Brace and Company, 1997), page 10.
6. Fred Heeren, quoting Albert Einstein, "What's Behind This 'Intelligent Design' Movement?" *Cosmic Pursuit,* Spring 1998, page 5.
7. Dillard, page 52.

Chapter 1: Our Body in Particles

1. Psalm 8:5; Hebrews 2:7.
2. David M. Baughan, M.D., "Contemporary Scientific Principles and Family Medicine," *Family Medicine,* volume 19, January/February 1987, page 42.
3. K. C. Cole, *The Universe and the Teacup: The Mathematics of Truth and Beauty* (San Diego: Harcourt Brace and Company, 1997), page 63.
4. "He is before all things, and in him all things hold together" (Colossians 1:17).
5. Shirley A. Jones (editor), quoting Sir J. Arthur Thomson, *The Mind of God & Other Musings: The Wisdom of Science* (San Rafael, CA: New World Library, 1994), pages 116-117.
6. Genesis 3:19.
7. Baughan, page 42.
8. Jones, quoting John Tyndall, page 96.
9. George Leonard, "In Praise of Monogamy," *American Health,* November 1988, page 105.

10. Lynn Margulis and Dorion Sagan, *Microcosmos* (New York: Summit Books, 1986), page 48.
11. 2 Corinthians 4:16.
12. The electric field is as large as 10^7 V/m. John R. Cameron, James G. Skofronick, and Roderick M. Grant, *Physics of the Body* (Madison, WI: Medical Physics Publishing, 1999), page 38: "Each of the trillions of living cells in the body has an electrical potential difference across the cell membrane. This is a result of an imbalance of the positively and negatively charged ions on the inside and outside of the cell wall. The resultant potential difference is about 0.1 V, but because of the very thin cell wall it may produce an electric field as large as 10^7 V/m, an electric field that is much larger than the electric field near a high voltage power line."
13. David Rosevear, "The Myth of Chemical Evolution," *Impact,* July 1999, page iv.
14. Rosevear, page iv.
15. Mark Caldwell, "The Clock in the Cell," *Discover,* October 1998, page 36.

Chapter 2: The Heart, Blood, and Lungs
1. John R. Cameron, James G. Skofronick, and Roderick M. Grant, *Physics of the Body* (Madison, WI: Medical Physics Publishing, 1999), page 191.
2. Ecclesiastes 3:11.
3. Laura D. Kubzansky et al., "A Prospective Study of Worry and Coronary Heart Disease in the Normative Aging Study," *Circulation,* 18 February 1997, pages 818-824.
4. Psalm 37:1-9.
5. Matthew 6:34.
6. Philippians 4:6.
7. Cameron et al., page 191.
8. Cameron et al., page 197: "The tension in a capillary wall is only about 24×10^{-3} N/m. For comparison, a single layer of toilet tissue can withstand a tension of about 50 N/m. This tension is about 3000 times greater than a tension which would rupture the capillary."
9. "For the life of a creature is in the blood, and I have given it to you to make atonement for yourselves on the altar; it is the blood that makes atonement for one's life" (Leviticus 17:11).
10. Fred Heeren, *Show Me God: What the Message from Space Is Telling Us About God* (Wheeling, IL: Day Star Publications, 1998), page 306.
11. The body can surge in two ways: it can begin releasing 100 percent of the oxygen molecules at the peripheral tissues instead of only 25 percent; in addition, it can greatly increase the cardiac output.
12. The blood contains twenty-five billion red blood cells per teaspoon.
13. Deuteronomy 5:29. Notice the position of this verse—just after a recounting of the Ten Commandments in Deuteronomy 5 and just before the *Shema* in Deuteronomy 6.
14. Paul Brand, M.D., and Philip Yancey, *Fearfully and Wonderfully Made* (Grand Rapids, MI: Zondervan, 1980), page 18.
15. Jeremy Rifkin, *Algeny* (New York: Viking, 1983), page 134.
16. Phillip F. Schewe and Ben Stein, "Physics News Update," *The American Institute of Physics Bulletin of Physics News,* number 394, 1 October 1998, http://newton.ex.ac.uk/aip/physnews.394.html (Physical Review Letters, 5 October 1998).
17. John 15:13.
18. Cameron et al., page 146: "Each time we breathe, a volume of about 0.5 liters containing ~10^{22} molecules of air enters our lungs. The total number of molecules in the earth's atmosphere is about 10^{44}. . . . For each molecule we breathe there are 10^{22} more in the earth's atmosphere. The earth's atmosphere is in constant motion, and over a period of centuries there has been thorough mixing of the gases. As a result, each breath, or 0.5 liter of air (10^{22} molecules), contains on the average one molecule that

was present in any 0.5 liter of air centuries ago. . . . On the average each of our breaths contains one air molecule that was in a single breath of Archimedes, Aristotle, or any other famous person who lived many years ago. Jesus Christ took approximately 150 million breaths in his lifetime; thus, one could expect that each of our breaths could contain about 150 million molecules breathed by Christ."

19. Daniel 5:23, RSV.
20. Genesis 2:7.
21. Cameron et al., page 147.
22. Psalm 150:6.

Chapter 3: The Senses

1. See 1 Corinthians 15:34.
2. George Ayoub, "On the Design of the Vertebrate Retina," *Origins & Design,* volume 17 number 1, 2 June 1999. Department of Biology, Westmont College, Santa Barbara, CA 93108-1099, Access Research Network, Analysis and Perspective.
3. Jeremy Rifkin, *Algeny* (New York: Viking, 1983), pages 139-140.
4. David Pescovitz, "Capturing Eyeballs under the Hood," *Wired,* September 1999, page 78.
5. Brad Stone, "Tired of All Those Passwords? There Are Some Alternatives," *Newsweek,* 30 November 1998, page 12.
6. John R. Cameron, James G. Skofronick, and Roderick M. Grant, *Physics of the Body* (Madison, WI: Medical Physics Publishing, 1999), page 321.
7. "Even the darkness will not be dark to you; the night will shine like the day, for darkness is as light to you" (Psalm 139:12).
8. Psalm 94:9, KJV.
9. John K. Stevens, "Reverse Engineering the Brain," *Byte,* April 1985, pages 287-299.
10. Shirley A. Jones (editor), quoting Gerhard Staguhn, *The Mind of God & Other Musings: The Wisdom of Science* (San Rafael, CA: New World Library, 1994), page 12.
11. Matthew 13:11-17.
12. Revelation 1:7.
13. Theodore Berland, *The Fight for Quiet* (Englewood Cliffs, NJ: Prentice-Hall, 1970), page 12.
14. Berland, page 7.
15. Cameron et al., page 276.
16. John Stott, quoting Leon Trotsky, *Issues Facing Christians Today: A Major Appraisal of Contemporary Social and Moral Questions* (Hants, UK: Marshall Morgan & Scott, 1984), page 139.
17. Gordon MacDonald, *Ordering Your Private World* (Nashville: Oliver-Nelson, 1985), page 126.
18. Dietrich Bonhoeffer, *Life Together* (New York: Harper & Brothers, 1954), pages 79-80.
19. Renee Solomon, "Mosquitoes also Prefer Attractive People—U.S. Study," Reuters Limited, AOL, 20 August 1999.
20. Richard Axel, "The Molecular Logic of Smell," *Scientific American,* October 1995, page 154.
21. Paul Brand, M.D., and Philip Yancey, *Fearfully and Wonderfully Made* (Grand Rapids, MI: Zondervan, 1980), pages 26 and 125.
22. 2 Corinthians 2:14-16.
23. Psalm 34:8; 1 Peter 2:2-3.
24. Isaiah 52:11.

Chapter 4: The Brain and Nervous System

1. Isaac Asimov, "In the Game of Energy & Thermodynamics You Can't Even Break Even," *Smithsonian Journal,* June 1970, page 10.

2. K. C. Cole, *The Universe and the Teacup: The Mathematics of Truth and Beauty* (San Diego, CA: Harcourt Brace and Company, 1997), page 24.

3. Don DeYoung and Richard Bliss, "Thinking about the Brain," *Impact,* February 1990, page ii.

4. Gerald L. Schroeder, *The Science of God: The Convergence of Scientific and Biblical Wisdom* (New York: Broadway Books, 1997), page 172.

5. W. Wayt Gibbs, "Dogma Overturned," *Scientific American,* November 1998, pages 19-20.

6. "Brain Food?" *U.S.News & World Report,* as quoted in *Signs of the Times,* September 1997, page 2.

7. N. Birbaumer et al., "A Spelling Device for the Paralyzed," *Nature,* volume 398, 25 March 1999, pages 297-298.

8. Sharon Begley, "Thinking Will Make It So," *Newsweek,* 5 April 1999, page 64.

9. Begley, page 64.

10. Begley, page 64.

11. Psalm 139:2,4.

12. C. S. Lewis, *Mere Christianity* (New York: Macmillan, 1952), pages 145-146.

13. Alan Lightman, "A Cataclysm of Thought," *The Atlantic Monthly,* January 1999, pages 89-96. Einstein had been unemployed much of the time since he graduated from the Federal Institute of Technology in Zurich in 1900, and in his "miraculous year" was working in a patent office in Bern, Switzerland. He had forsaken his German citizenship over political and military disagreements.

14. Darold A. Treffert, M.D., *Extraordinary People: Understanding Savant Syndrome* (New York: Ballantine Books, 1989), page 13.

15. Treffert, pages 1,2,59.

16. Anthony Smith, *Intimate Universe: The Human Body* (London: BBC Books, 1998), page 152.

17. Jeremy Campbell, *Grammatical Man: Information, Entropy, Language, and Life* (New York: Simon & Schuster, 1982), pages 222-224.

18. Rob Parsons, "Almost Everything I Need to Know About God I Learned in Sunday School," *Focus on the Family,* February 2000, page 6.

19. Irving Dardik, M.D., and Denis Waitley, *Quantum Fitness—Breakthrough to Excellence* (New York: Simon & Schuster, 1984), page 27.

20. Vincent Ryan Ruggiero, *The Art of Thinking: A Guide to Critical and Creative Thought* (New York: Harper & Row, 1988), page 3.

21. Campbell, pages 222 and 227.

22. Daniel J. Boorstin, *The Discoverers* (New York: Random House, 1983), page 487.

23. Boorstin, quoting William James, page 488.

24. 1 Corinthians 13:5.

25. Jeremiah 31:34 (the sentiment is echoed in Psalm 103 and Isaiah 43:25, among many other places in the Bible).

26. Deuteronomy 5:15.

27. Psalm 105:4-5.

28. Dardik and Waitley, page 13.

29. David G. Myers, "Yin and Yang in Psychological Research and Christian Belief," *Perspectives on Science and Christian Faith,* volume 39, number 3, September 1987, page 134.

30. Joseph M. Mercola, *Healthy News You Can Use,* Issue 100, 9 May 1999, drawing from Kourosh Saberi and David R. Perrott, "Cognitive Restoration of Reversed Speech," *Nature,* volume 398, 29 April 1999, page 760.

31. James 3:9.

32. J. Christian Gillin, M.D., and William F. Byerley, M.D., "The Diagnosis and Management of Insomnia," *The New England Journal of Medicine,* volume 322, number 4, 1990, page 239.

33. Psalm 16:7.

34. "Sleep Problems Are Pervasive: Poll Finds," *American Medical News,* 12 April 1999, pages 51,54,56.
35. "Basic Sleep 101, or You Have to Be Awake to Fall Asleep," Land and Sky website, http://www.landandsky.com/technology.html.
36. Psalm 127:2.
37. Mark Looy, quoting Michael Denton, *Evolution: A Theory in Crisis* (London: Burnett Books, Ltd., 1985), page 331, in "I Think; Therefore, There Is a Supreme Thinker," *Impact,* October 1990, page ii.
38. Otis Port, "21 Ideas for the 21st Century: Humanity—#7. The Mind Is Immortal," *Business Week,* 30 August 1999.
39. Todd Siler, *Breaking the Mind Barrier: A Brilliantly Original Way to Think about Art, Science, the Mind, and the Universe* (New York: Touchstone, 1992), page 195.
40. 2 Corinthians 10:5.
41. Carl F. H. Henry, *Christian Countermoves in a Decadent Culture* (Portland, OR: Multnomah Press, 1986), page 144.
42. 1 Corinthians 1:19.
43. A. W. Tozer, *Born After Midnight* (Camp Hill, PA: Christian Publications, 1992), page 62.
44. 1 Corinthians 1:21.
45. Psalm 111:10.
46. 1 Corinthians 1:20.
47. Isaiah 47:10.
48. 1 Corinthians 13:2.
49. 2 Timothy 3:1-2,7.
50. John 17:17.
51. Ephesians 1:17-18, KJV.
52. 1 Corinthians 8:1.
53. Thomas Stearns Eliot, *The Rock,* a verse play, 1934.
54. Paul Johnson, "Beware the Intellectuals: The High Priests of Knowledge," *U.S.News & World Report,* 27 March 1989, page 73.
55. "Science Can't Explain 'Who Am I? Why Am I Here?'" A Conversation with Sir John Eccles, *U.S.News & World Report,* 1984, page 80.
56. Dana Ullman, quoting Lyall Watson, "Psychological Problems: Treating Mind and Body," in *Discovering Homeopathy: Medicine for the 21st Century* (Berkeley, CA: North Atlantic, 1991), taken from the Internet.

Chapter 5: The Cell, Genes, and DNA

1. Authorities vary in their estimates from 10 to 100 trillion cells in the human body.
2. Gerald L. Schroeder, *The Science of God: The Convergence of Scientific and Biblical Wisdom* (New York: Broadway Books, 1997), page 142.
3. Anthony Smith, *Intimate Universe: The Human Body* (London: BBC Books, 1998), page 11.
4. In the United States, the Human Genome Project is jointly funded by the Department of Energy (DOE) and the National Institutes of Health (NIH). The DOE-funded participants include the Joint Genome Institute, the University of Washington, and the Institute for Genomic Research. The NIH-funded participants include Washington University (St. Louis), Massachusetts Institute of Technology, Baylor University, University of Washington, University of Texas Southwestern Medical Center, Stanford University, and the University of Oklahoma. In addition, the United Kingdom, Germany, and Japan are making major contributions to the program, along with fourteen other countries.
5. A is adenine, C is cytidine, G is guanine, and T is thymine.
6. "Primer on Molecular Genetics," Human Genome Project Information website, http://www.ornl.gov/hgmis/publicat/primer/prim1.html.
7. "Primer on Molecular Genetics."

8. Alma E. Guinness (editor), *ABC's of the Human Body* (Pleasantville, NY: The Reader's Digest Association, Inc., 1987), page 38. Every human cell is thought to contain up to 6 feet of DNA, which adds up to 17 billion miles in the whole body. One scientist has described DNA as an "exquisitely thin filament," so light that a thread of it running all the way from the earth to the sun would weigh only .02 ounce.

9. Paul Brand, M.D., and Philip Yancey, *Fearfully and Wonderfully Made* (Grand Rapids, MI: Zondervan, 1980), page 46.

10. Measurements about how long the DNA from an individual cell is range from 5 to 9 feet. Estimates of the total number of cells in a human body range from 10 to 100 trillion. Thus the lower end for total length of DNA is 5 feet x 10 trillion; the upper end is 9 feet x 100 trillion.

11. Michael Behe, "Molecular Machines," *Cosmic Pursuit*, Spring 1998, page 30.

12. Shirley A. Jones (editor), quoting Maxine Singer, *The Mind of God & Other Musings: The Wisdom of Science* (San Rafael, CA: New World Library, 1994), page 117.

13. This material can be found on the Human Genome Project Information website at http://www.ornl.gov/hgmis/faq/faqs1.html.

14. Clifford A. Pickover, *Keys to Infinity* (New York: John Wiley & Sons, Inc., 1995), page 127.

15. "Gene Therapy—An Overview," Access Excellence website, Genentech, http://www.accessexcellence.org/AB/IWT/Gene_Therapy_Overview.html, 1998.

16. Fred Heeren, quoting Michael Denton, *Evolution: A Theory in Crisis* (Bethesda, MD: Adler & Adler Publishers, Inc., 1986), pages 249-250, in "Exoplanets, SETI, and the Likelihood of Contact," *Cosmic Pursuit*, Spring 1999, page 58.

17. Schroeder, page 83; quoting George Wald, "The Origin of Life," *Scientific American*, August 1954.

18. Schroeder, page 84; quoting C. Folsome, *Life: Origin and Evolution*, Scientific American Special Publication, 1979.

19. Schroeder, page 124.

20. J. P. Moreland (editor), quoting Marcel P. Schutzenberger from "Algorithms and the Neo-Darwinian Theory of Evolution," in the John Ankerberg and John Weldon chapter "Rational Inquiry & the Force of Scientific Data: Are New Horizons Emerging?" *The Creation Hypothesis: Scientific Evidence for an Intelligent Designer* (Downers Grove, IL: InterVarsity, 1994), page 274.

21. Hugh Ross, quoting Harold Morowitz, *The Creator and the Cosmos: How the Greatest Scientific Discoveries of the Century Reveal God* (Colorado Springs, CO: NavPress, 1995), page 149.

22. Fred Heeren, quoting Edward Argyle from "Chance and the Origin of Life," *Extraterrestrials—Where are They?*, Ben Zuckerman and Michael H. Hart (editors) (Cambridge, England: Cambridge University Press, 1995), page 131, in *Show Me God: What the Message from Space Is Telling Us About God* (Wheeling, IL: Day Star Publications, 1998), page 61.

23. Schroeder, quoting John Horgan, page 85.

24. Heeren, quoting Fred Hoyle and Chandra Wickramasinghe, from *Evolution from Space* (London: J. M. Dent and Sons, 1981), page 24, in *Show Me God*, page 209.

25. Heeren, quoting David Foster, *Show Me God*, page 68.

26. Heeren, quoting Fred Hoyle and Chandra Wickramasinghe, from *Evolution from Space*, page 148 (see note 24), in *Show Me God*, page 68.

27. Schroeder, page 93.

28. Schroeder, page 102.

29. J. P. Moreland (editor), quoting Carl Sagan and Francis Crick in the John Ankerberg and John Weldon chapter "Rational Inquiry & the Force of Scientific Data: Are New Horizons Emerging?" *The Creation Hypothesis: Scientific Evidence for an Intelligent Designer* (Downers Grove, IL: InterVarsity, 1994), page 272.

30. Stephen C. Meyer, "The Message in the Microcosm: DNA and the Death of Materialism," *Cosmic Pursuit*, Fall 1997, pages 41-42.
31. Meyer, pages 43-45.
32. "Once to Every Man and Nation," poem by James Russell Lowell, 1819–1891.
33. Leon Jaroff, "Fixing the Genes," *Time*, 11 January 1999, page 68.
34. Frederic Golden, "Good Eggs, Bad Eggs," *Time*, 11 January 1999, page 58.
35. Laurie McGinley and Anne Fawcett, "Patients and Abortion Foes Clash on Stem-Cell Research," *The Wall Street Journal*, 21 June 1999, page A28. And "Geron Research Reproduces 'Immortal' Human Stem Cells," *Bloomberg News*, 10 November 1998, taken from the Internet.
36. "Gene Therapy—An Overview," Access Excellence website, Genentech, http://www.accessexcellence.org/AB/IWT/Gene_Therapy_Overview.html, 1998.
37. John Carey, quoting Lee Silver, "We'll Have All the Genetic Pieces. Next, We'll Assemble the Jigsaw Puzzle," *Business Week*, 30 August 1999, taken from the Internet.
38. Sharon Begley with Thomas Hayden, "How Low Can You Go?" *Newsweek*, 22 February 1999, page 50.
39. J. Madeleine Nash, "The Age of Cloning," *Time*, 10 March 1997, page 64.
40. Gene Edward Veith, "Birds, Bees, and Bovine," *World*, 14 February 1998, page 24.
41. "Advanced Cell Technology Announces Use of Nuclear Transfer Technology for Successful Generation of Human Embryonic Stem Cells," Advanced Cell Technology, Inc. website, http://www.advancedcell.com/PR111298.htm, 12 November 1998.
42. "Rael Creates the First Human Cloning Company," Clonaid website, http://www.clonaid.com.

Chapter 6: The Skin, Stomach, Skeleton, and Sperm

1. Paul Brand, M.D., and Philip Yancey, *Fearfully and Wonderfully Made* (Grand Rapids, MI: Zondervan, 1980), page 151.
2. John Medina, "Time and the Search for Significance," seminar given at University Presbyterian Church, Seattle, WA, 26 February 1997.
3. Jeremiah 6:15.
4. Exodus 34:29-35, KJV.
5. Genesis 3:19.
6. 1 Peter 3:3-4.
7. Isaac Bashevis Singer, *The Penitent* (New York: Farrar, Straus, Giroux, 1983), page 122.
8. Job 19:20.
9. Tim Friend, "Everest Tops Out: Add 7 Feet," *USA Today*, 12 November 1999, page 1A.
10. 1 Corinthians 10:12, RSV.
11. Psalm 3:7, NIV, 1978.
12. Luke 20:18.
13. Matthew 8:12; 22:13; 24:51; 25:30.
14. John R. Cameron, James G. Skofronick, and Roderick M. Grant, *Physics of the Body* (Madison, WI: Medical Physics Publishing, 1999), page 17.
15. Michael D. Gershon, "The Enteric Nervous System: A Second Brain," *Hospital Practice*, 15 July 1999, page 31.
16. "Your Liver, A Vital Organ," American Liver Foundation website, http://gi.ucsf.edu/alf/info/infovital.html, 1997.
17. Anna Mae Diehl, M.D., and Clifford Steer, M.D., "Liver Regeneration," American Liver Foundation website, http://gi.ucsf.edu/alf/pubs/progregen.html, 1996, page 1.
18. Diehl and Steer, page 1.
19. "Reflections," quoting C. S. Lewis in *Mere Christianity*, *Christianity Today*, 11 January 1999, page 80.
20. John 4:32,34.
21. Cameron et al., page 96.

22. Brand and Yancey, page 70.
23. Cameron et al., page 98.
24. K. C. Cole, *The Universe and the Teacup: The Mathematics of Truth and Beauty* (San Diego: Harcourt Brace and Company, 1997), pages 54-55.
25. "Bone Physiology—Remodeling," University of Washington website, http://courses.washington.edu/bonephys/physiology.html.
26. Carolyn J. Strange, "Boning Up on Osteoporosis," U.S. Food and Drug Administration website, Publication No. 97-1257 (FDA), http://www.fda.gov/fdac/features/796_bone.html, August 1997, page 2.
27. Cameron et al., page 91.
28. Dan Cray, "NASA Builds Muscles," *Time,* 22 March 1999, page 88.
29. Psalm 139:14.
30. Job 10:8,12.
31. Alma E. Guinness (editor), *ABC's of the Human Body* (Pleasantville, NY: The Reader's Digest Association, Inc., 1987), page 270.
32. Anthony Smith, *Intimate Universe: The Human Body* (London: BBC Books, 1998), page 27.
33. Psalm 139:13.

Chapter 7: Our Body, His Temple
1. Genesis 1:26.
2. Psalm 8:5; Hebrews 2:7.
3. 1 Corinthians 6:19-20.
4. Romans 12:1.
5. Luke 1:30,32.
6. Philippians 2:5-7.
7. Romans 12:4-5.

Chapter 8: Energy, Force, Matter, and God
1. Hugh Ross, quoting Robert Griffiths, *The Creator and the Cosmos: How the Greatest Scientific Discoveries of the Century Reveal God* (Colorado Springs, CO: NavPress, 1995), page 123.
2. Owen Gingerich, quoting Fred Hoyle, in "Let There Be Light: Modern Cosmogony and Biblical Creation," Timothy Ferris (editor), *The World Treasury of Physics, Astronomy, and Mathematics* (Boston: Little, Brown and Company, 1991), pages 392-393.
3. Schrödinger's cat is a famous example of the indeterminism built into quantum physics. The cat is in an opaque box with a random radioactive decay switching device. If the decay randomly triggers one switch, the cat will be fed food and live. If the decay randomly triggers the other switch, the cat will be fed poison and die. Schrödinger's point is that within the strange quantum world of random indeterminism, the cat is both dead and alive. Once we open the box, the cat will be *either* dead or alive. But before we open the box, the cat is *both* dead and alive *at the same time.*
4. Clifford A. Pickover, quoting Roger Shepard, *Keys to Infinity* (New York: John Wiley & Sons, Inc., 1995), page xvii.
5. Paul Davies, quoting Fred Hoyle, *The Mind of God: The Scientific Basis for a Rational World* (New York: Simon & Schuster, 1993), page 22.
6. Ian Marshall and Danah Zohar, *Who's Afraid of Schrödinger's Cat? An A-to-Z Guide to All the New Science Ideas You Need to Keep Up with the New Thinking* (New York: William Morrow, 1997), page 5.
7. Robert C. Weast (editor in chief), *Handbook of Chemistry and Physics* (Cleveland: The Chemical Rubber Co., 1964), page B-105.
8. Robert P. Kirshner, "The Earth's Elements," *Scientific American,* October 1994, page 49.
9. K. C. Cole, quoting Arthur Eddington, *The Universe and the Teacup: The Mathematics of Truth and Beauty* (San Diego: Harcourt Brace and Company, 1997), page 46.

10. Davies, page 85.
11. *Encyclopaedia Britannica*, 15th ed., s.v. "atom."
12. Brian Greene, quoting Isidor Isaac Rabi, *The Elegant Universe: Superstrings, Hidden Dimensions, and the Quest for the Ultimate Theory* (New York: W. W. Norton & Company, 1999), page 8.
13. Shirley A. Jones (editor), quoting Gerhard Staguhn, *The Mind of God & Other Musings: The Wisdom of Science* (San Rafael, CA: New World Library, 1994), page 49.
14. Timothy Ferris (editor), *The World Treasury of Physics, Astronomy, and Mathematics* (Boston: Little, Brown and Company, 1991), page 1.
15. "RHIC [Relativistic Heavy Ion Collider] Physics Primer," Relativistic Heavy Ion Collider website, http://www.rhic.bnl.gov/html2/primer.html, 11 December 1999.
16. Jones, quoting Gerhard Staguhn, page 49.
17. Edward Kearns, Takaaki Kajita, and Yoji Totsuka, "Detecting Massive Neutrinos," *Scientific American,* August 1999, page 66.
18. Kearns et al., page 70.
19. "Fascinating RHIC Facts," Relativistic Heavy Ion Collider website, http://www.rhic.bnl.gov/html2/facts.html, 11 December 1999.
20. "Committee Report on Speculative 'Disaster Scenarios' at RHIC," Brookhaven National Laboratory (BNL) website, http://www.bnl.gov/bnlweb/rhicreport.html, 11 December 1999. Opinion written 6 October 1999.
21. "Introduction," Antimatter Space Propulsion at Penn State University (LEPS), http://antimatter.phys.psu.edu/introduction.html, 11 December 1999.
22. "The pillars of heaven tremble and are astonished at his reproof" (Job 26:11, KJV). "The mountains melt like wax before the Lord" (Psalm 97:5, NIV). "The hills melted like wax at the presence of the Lord" (Psalm 97:5, KJV).
23. Gerald L. Schroeder, *The Science of God: The Convergence of Scientific and Biblical Wisdom* (New York: Broadway Books, 1997), page 186.
24. Clifford A. Pickover, *Time: A Traveler's Guide* (New York: Oxford University Press, 1998), pages 136-137.
25. Hugh Ross, *Beyond the Cosmos: What Recent Discoveries in Astronomy and Physics Reveal About the Nature of God* (Colorado Springs, CO: NavPress, 1996), pages 196-197.
26. Hans C. von Baeyer, *Rainbows, Snowflakes and Quarks: Physics and the World Around Us* (New York: McGraw-Hill, 1984), pages 26-27.
27. Robert Wearner, "Newton: Man of the Future," *Signs of the Times,* February 1999, page 27; quoting I. Bernard Cohen, "Isaac Newton's Papers and Letters on Natural Philosophy," page 928.
28. Stephen Hawking, interview by Kathy A. Svitil, "Hawking's Vision: The All-in-One Theory," *Discover,* March 1999, page 18.
29. Stephen Hawking, *A Brief History of Time: From the Big Bang to Black Holes* (New York: Bantam Books, 1988), page 175.
30. Jones, quoting Stephen Hawking, page 52.
31. John Gribbin, *Q is for Quantum: An Encyclopedia of Particle Physics* (New York: The Free Press of Simon & Schuster, 1998), pages 139-140, 150-151.
32. Acts 17:27.

Chapter 9: The New Physics

1. Gerald L. Schroeder, *The Science of God: The Convergence of Scientific and Biblical Wisdom* (New York: Broadway Books, 1997), page 1. The universe is thought to contain 10^{56} grams of matter, which equals 10^{50} tons.
2. Karl W. Giberson, "Much Ado about Nada," *Books & Culture,* January/February 2000, page 34.
3. Paul Davies, *The Mind of God: The Scientific Basis for a Rational World* (New York: Simon & Schuster, 1993), page 47.

4. Alan Lightman, "A Cataclysm of Thought," *The Atlantic Monthly*, January 1999, page 89.

5. Lightman, page 94.

6. Tony Augarde (editor), quoting Albert Einstein from his address at the Sorbonne, Paris, December 1929, in *New York Times*, 16 February 1930, in *The Oxford Dictionary of Modern Quotations* (New York: Oxford University Press, 1991), page 73.

7. Hugh Ross, *Beyond the Cosmos: What Recent Discoveries in Astronomy and Physics Reveal About the Nature of God* (Colorado Springs, CO: NavPress, 1996), pages 35-36.

8. "God is light; in him there is no darkness at all" (1 John 1:5). "[Jesus] said, 'I am the light of the world'" (John 8:12).

9. Ian Marshall and Danah Zohar, *Who's Afraid of Schrödinger's Cat? An A-to-Z Guide to All the New Science Ideas You Need to Keep Up with the New Thinking* (New York: William Morrow, 1997), page 295.

10. Brian Greene, *The Elegant Universe: Superstrings, Hidden Dimensions, and the Quest for the Ultimate Theory* (New York: W. W. Norton & Company, 1999), page 87.

11. James Gleick, quoting Richard Feynman, *Genius: The Life and Science of Richard Feynman* (New York: Vintage Books, 1992), page 13.

12. Robert L. Herrmann and John M. Templeton, "Scientific Contributions to Meaning and Purpose in the Universe," *Perspectives on Science and Christian Faith*, June 1987, page 84.

13. Greene, quoting Richard Feynman, pages 86-87.

14. David J. Chalmers, *The Conscious Mind: In Search of a Fundamental Theory* (New York: Oxford University Press, 1996), page 356.

15. Chalmers, page 335.

16. Chalmers, page 342.

17. Marshall and Zohar, page 297.

18. Ian Stewart, *Life's Other Secret: The New Mathematics of the Living World* (New York: John Wiley & Sons, Inc., 1998), page 8.

19. Greene, page 114.

20. Ross, page 37.

21. Greene, pages 118 and 150.

22. Marshall and Zohar, page 201.

23. Frederic Golden, "Person of the Century: Albert Einstein," *Time*, 31 December 1999, page 58.

24. Herrmann and Templeton, page 84.

25. Don B. DeYoung, "Creation and Quantum Mechanics," *Impact*, November 1998, page iv.

26. Freeman J. Dyson, *Infinite in All Directions* (New York: Harper & Row, 1988), page 18.

27. John Horgan, *The End of Science: Facing the Limits of Knowledge in the Twilight of the Scientific Age* (Reading, MA: Addison-Wesley, 1996), page 62.

28. 1 Corinthians 2:9, NEB.

29. Shirley A. Jones (editor), quoting Gerhard Staguhn, *The Mind of God & Other Musings: The Wisdom of Science* (San Rafael, CA: New World Library, 1994), page 17.

Chapter 10: The Story of the Stars

1. Shirley Jones (editor), quoting Gerhard Staguhn, *The Mind of God & Other Musings: The Wisdom of Science* (San Rafael, CA: New World Library, 1994), page 12.

2. Isaiah 40:26.

3. "Reflections," quoting John Glenn, *Christianity Today*, 11 January 1999, page 80.

4. George F. Will, "The Gospel from Science," *Newsweek*, 9 November 1998, page 88.

5. "Do you not know? Have you not heard? The LORD is the everlasting God, the Creator of the ends of the earth. He will not grow tired or weary, and his understanding no one can fathom" (Isaiah 40:28).

6. Sharon Begley, quoting Joel Primack, "Science Finds God," *Newsweek*, 20 July 1998, page 50.

7. Fred Heeren, quoting Stephen Hawking, *Show Me God: What the Message from Space Is Telling Us About God* (Wheeling, IL: Day Star Publications, 1998), page 377.

8. Cathy Lynn Grossman, quoting Steven Weinberg, "Scientists, theologians wrestle with eternal questions of God," *USA Today,* 20 April 1999, page 9D.

9. Jones, quoting Steven Weinberg, page 11.

10. Begley, quoting Charles Townes, page 49.

11. Begley, quoting Allan Sandage, page 46.

12. Fred Heeren, quoting Allan Sandage, "The Great Debate," *Cosmic Pursuit,* Fall 1997, page 11.

13. Leland Ryken, quoting Gerard Manley Hopkins, "The Creative Arts," chapter in *The Making of a Christian Mind: A Christian World View & the Academic Enterprise,* edited by Arthur Holmes (Downers Grove, IL: InterVarsity, 1985), page 123.

14. Todd Siler, quoting Virginia Trimble, *Breaking the Mind Barrier: A Brilliantly Original Way to Think about Art, Science, the Mind, and the Universe* (New York: Simon & Schuster, 1990), page 59.

15. Psalm 147:4.

16. Philippians 2:15.

17. K. C. Cole, *The Universe and the Teacup: The Mathematics of Truth and Beauty* (San Diego: Harcourt Brace and Company, 1997), pages 49-50.

18. Robert I. Fitzhenry (editor), quoting G. K. Chesterton, *Barnes & Noble Book of Quotations* (New York: HarperCollins, 1987), page 321.

19. Genesis 1:16 and Revelation 22:16.

20. Lambert Dolphin, *Lord of Time and Space* (Westchester, IL: Good News Publishers, 1974), page 22.

21. Roy A. Gallant, *Our Universe* (Washington, DC: National Geographic Society, 1986), page 63.

22. Cole, quoting Sir James Jeans, page 20.

23. Jones, quoting David E. Lilienthal, page 15.

24. Poem by M. D. Babcock.

25. Bob Berman, "Twilight Zone," *Discover,* March 1999, page 129.

26. Hugh Ross, *The Creator and the Cosmos: How the Greatest Scientific Discoveries of the Century Reveal God* (Colorado Springs, CO: NavPress, 1995), page 135.

27. Fred Heeren, "Exoplanets, SETI, and the Likelihood of Contact," *Cosmic Pursuit,* Spring 1999, page 27.

28. Peter D. Ward and Donald Brownlee, *Rare Earth: Why Complex Life Is Uncommon in the Universe* (New York: Copernicus, Springer-Verlag, 2000), pages 240,51,37.

29. Ward and Brownlee, pages 37 and 265.

30. Ross, page 137.

31. Yotta is the prefix for 10^{24}—a number arbitrarily chosen for whimsical reasons.

32. Freeman J. Dyson, *Infinite in All Directions* (New York: Harper & Row, 1988), page 20.

33. Clifford A. Pickover, quoting Richard Gott, *Time: A Traveler's Guide* (New York: Oxford University Press, 1998), page 134.

34. Brian Greene, *The Elegant Universe: Superstrings, Hidden Dimensions, and the Quest for the Ultimate Theory* (New York: W. W. Norton & Company, 1999), page 80.

35. Clifford A. Pickover, *Black Holes: A Traveler's Guide* (New York: John Wiley & Sons, Inc., 1996), page 22.

36. Pickover, *Black Holes,* page xi.

37. Jean-Pierre Lasota, "Unmasking Black Holes," *Scientific American,* May 1999, pages 41-42.

38. Phillip F. Schewe and Ben Stein, "Physics News Update," *The American Institute of Physics Bulletin of Physics News,* Number 394, 1 October 1998, by http://www.netwon.ex.ac.uk/aip/physnews.394.html (Physical Review Letters, 5 October 1998).

39. Thomas Hayden, "Debut of a Mighty Magnetar," *Newsweek,* 12 October 1998, page 73.

40. Michael D. Lemonick, "Close Encounter with a Comet," *Time,* 8 February 1999, page 50.

41. "Earth-Crossing Asteroids," University of Tennessee Astronomy Department website, http://csep10.phys.utk.edu/astr161/lect/asteroids/collisions.html.
42. Marc G. Millis, "Warp Drive, When?—Ideas Based on What We'd Like To Achieve," NASA Breakthrough Physics Program Public Information Site, http://www.lerc.nasa.gov/WWW/PAO/html/warp/ideachev.htm.
43. Jeremiah 32:17.
44. Hugh Ross, interview, "Scientists Are Getting Warmer," *New Man,* September/October 1999, page 34.

Chapter 11: Time, Space, and Light

1. 1 Corinthians 13:12, KJV.
2. Clifford A. Pickover, *Time: A Traveler's Guide* (New York: Oxford University Press, 1998), pages 58-59.
3. Pickover, *Time: A Traveler's Guide,* page 41.
4. C. S. Lewis, *Mere Christianity* (New York: MacMillan, 1952), page 146; and Lambert Dolphin, Jr., *Lord of Space and Time* (Westchester, IL: Good News Publishers, 1974), pages 47-48.
5. Lewis, pages 148-149.
6. James 4:14.
7. "You have made my days a mere handbreadth; the span of my years is as nothing before you. Each man's life is but a breath" (Psalm 39:5).
8. 2 Corinthians 4:17.
9. A. W. Tozer (editor), quoting Frederick William Faber, *The Christian Book of Mystical Verse* (Harrisburg, PA: Christian Publications, Inc., 1963), page 14. The poem is composed of fourteen stanzas, of which only two are quoted in this chapter.
10. Pickover, quoting Albert Einstein, *Time: A Traveler's Guide,* page 6.
11. Doug Trouten, "Celtic Spirituality," *Minnesota Christian Chronicle,* 18 March 1999, page 1; quoting Steve Rabey, *In the House of Memory: Ancient Celtic Wisdom for Everyday Life* (New York: Dutton, 1998), page 5.
12. Clifford A. Pickover, quoting Woody Allen, *Black Holes: A Traveler's Guide* (New York: John Wiley & Sons, Inc., 1996), page 40.
13. Todd Siler, quoting Saint Augustine in *Confessions, Breaking the Mind Barrier: A Brilliantly Original Way to Think about Art, Science, the Mind, and the Universe* (New York: Simon & Schuster, 1990), page 287.
14. Laura Ingalls Wilder, *Little House in the Big Woods* (New York: Harper & Row Publishers, 1953), page 238.
15. Dolphin, page 64.
16. Clifford A. Pickover, *Keys to Infinity* (New York: John Wiley & Sons, Inc., 1995), page xiii. The quotation is from a 1921 history book, *The Story of Mankind,* by Hendrik Willem Van Loon, who starts his book with the parable quoted.
17. Fred Heeren and Bernard Leikind, "The Great Debate: Is There Now Scientific Evidence for God? Yes! Fred Heeren No! Bernard Leikind," *Cosmic Pursuit,* Fall 1997, page 23.
18. John D. Barrow, quoting George Bernard Shaw, *Theories of Everything: The Quest for Ultimate Explanation* (New York: Oxford University Press, 1991), page 54.
19. John Piper, "He Commanded and They Were Created," Bethlehem Baptist Church, St. Paul, MN, sermon notes for 4 October 1981, pages 2 and 4.
20. Luke 24:31.
21. Acts 8:39.
22. Matthew 14:25-26.
23. John 20:19,26.
24. Hugh Ross, *Beyond the Cosmos: What Recent Discoveries in Astronomy and Physics Reveal About the Nature of God* (Colorado Springs, CO: NavPress, 1996), page 46.

25. K. C. Cole, *The Universe and the Teacup: The Mathematics of Truth and Beauty* (San Diego: Harcourt Brace and Company, 1997), page 58.

26. Cole, page 196.

27. Douglas Adams, *The Hitchhiker's Guide to the Galaxy* (New York: Ballantine Books, 1980), pages 195-196.

28. John R. Cameron, James G. Skofronick, and Roderick M. Grant, *Physics of the Body* (Madison, WI: Medical Physics Publishing, 1999), page 321.

29. Gerald L. Schroeder, *The Science of God: The Convergence of Scientific and Biblical Wisdom* (New York: Broadway Books, 1997), page 155.

30. John Gribbin, *Q is for Quantum: An Encyclopedia of Particle Physics* (New York: The Free Press of Simon & Schuster, 1998), page 283.

31. Brian Greene, *The Elegant Universe: Superstrings, Hidden Dimensions, and the Quest for the Ultimate Theory* (New York: W. W. Norton & Company, 1999), page 51.

32. Schroeder, page 162.

33. Schroeder, page 164.

34. Pickover, *Time: A Traveler's Guide,* page 181.

35. Poem by Walter Chalmers Smith (1824–1908).

36. Tozer, quoting Thomas Blacklock's poem "Come, O My Soul," page 83.

37. Tozer, quoting William Cowper's poem "Sometimes A Light Surprises," pages 71-72.

38. Genesis 1:3.

39. Revelation 22:5.

40. John 8:12.

41. 1 John 1:5.

42. Revelation 21:23-25.

Chapter 12: Science, Scripture, and Sovereignty

1. Matthew 13:11.

2. Luke 7:16.

3. Matthew 9:33.

4. Mark 7:37.

5. Mark 1:27.

6. Luke 9:43; Mark 2:12; Luke 5:26.

7. Matthew 8:19.

8. Luke 5:8.

9. John 1:49.

10. John 1:29.

11. John 12:19.

12. Luke 8:25.

13. Mark 1:36-37.

14. Matthew 14:26,33.

15. Luke 2:47.

16. John 7:15.

17. Mark 12:37.

18. Matthew 7:29.

19. Luke 4:20,22.

20. John 4:29,42.

21. John 12:13.

22. John 7:45-46.

23. Luke 23:8.

24. Mark 15:39.

25. Luke 24:32.

26. Malcolm Muggeridge, *Jesus: The Man Who Lives* (New York: Harper & Row Publishers, 1975), page 74.

27. Clifford A. Pickover, *Keys to Infinity* (New York: John Wiley & Sons, Inc., 1995), page 193.
28. Michael J. Behe, "Tulips & Dandelions," *Books & Culture,* September/October 1998, page 34. [The British mathematician is Oxford University's renowned Roger Penrose.]
29. Russ Johnston, "Faith That Works," *Discipleship Journal,* issue 3, page 5.
30. Matthew 17:20, RSV.
31. George Croly (1780–1860), "Spirit of God, Descend upon My Heart."

INDEX

About *the* Author

RICHARD A. SWENSON, M.D. is a physician and futurist, with a B.S. in physics Phi Beta Kappa from Denison University and an M.D. from the University of Illinois School of Medicine. Following fifteen years teaching with the University of Wisconsin Medical School, Dr. Swenson currently researches and writes full-time about the intersection of culture, health, faith, and the future. He is a highly requested speaker on the implications of societal change to a variety of audiences, including career, professional, and management groups; major church denominations; members of Congress; and the Pentagon.

Dr. Swenson and his wife, Linda, live in Menomonie, Wisconsin, with their two sons, Adam and Matthew.